The Color Treasury of Gemstones

The Color Treasury of

GEMSTONES

Text by Dr. Eduard Gübelin, Gemmologist, C.G. F.G.A.

Photographs by Michael Wolgensinger and Dr. Eduard Gübelin

THOMAS Y. CROWELL COMPANY

Established 1834 New York

The author sincerely wishes to thank all those listed below who have helped him in the preparation of this book: Michael Wolgensinger for his cooperation in the production of the full-page color plates; Dr. H. Bank and W. Fink for placing at the author's disposal countless rough specimens, crystals, and cut stones; Dr. H. Bank and J. Ryser for providing Figs. 31, 32, 55, 57, and 58; as well as F. Klein for the original of Fig. 7; M. Burch for the loan of some of the jewelry in Figs. 30, 36, 44, 50, 54, 56, and 59; P. Binder for that of the ornamental pieces in Plate 43; and Miss P. B. Lapworth for her excellent translation from the German text, in which she grasped particularly well the rather difficult poetical sense.

Originally published in German as *Edelsteine*.

Translation copyright © 1975 by
Thomas Y. Crowell Company, Inc.

Copyright © 1969 by Silva-Verlag, Zürich

Designed by Abigail Moseley

PRINTED IN BELGIUM
by OFFSET VAN DEN BOSSCHE

Library of Congress Cataloging in Publication Data

Gübelin, Eduard Josef, 1913–
    The color treasury of gemstones.

    1. Precious stones—Pictorial works.
I. Wolgensinger, Michael. II. Title.
QE392.G79   553'.8   75–15715
ISBN 0–690–00986–0

1   2   3   4   5   6   7   8   9   10

Contents

A Song in Praise of Gemstones

THIS book sets out no specialized arcane knowledge. The layman will hardly be burdened with the all-too-tedious data on physical properties. This book attempts, rather, to provide—with a touch of poetry—a comprehensive and easily accessible survey of the gemstone realm. No one will be surprised if women are especially attracted to it. For who, if not Woman, is fitted to form the appropriate setting for the magical play of choice jewels? May the verses of the poet Friedrich Rückert introduce the gemstone to you as one of Nature's most precious and beautiful wonders:

Behold the gemstone—how firmly built and fast!
Impenetrable, and from a sole piece cast!

Yet acorns 'gainst foreign forces its doors to fasten tight,
For the Impenetrable is traversed by glowing warmth and light.

And its very color, soaked up as it wills,
By turns is dull now, and then with splendor fills.

Now flares, now wanes, in every tint and hue,
And flashes different fire from different points of view.

A cloudlet floating in its depths, you find,
Alters its place—and wonder grips your mind.

But wonder not; rather a lesson learn
From gemstones—like them, be steadfast and be firm.

No heart can be so numbly within itself enfurled
As never to be softened by sympathy for the world.

Be hard as gems, but also be as pure,
And ornament God's garden where only they endure.

Flowers of the Mineral Kingdom

WHILE man has been able to decipher most of the life secrets of animals and flowers, gemstones—the beguiling children of the great mineral kingdom—have remained a secret, just like the biblical seven seals, to many admirers of our manifold creation. The author hopes that he will succeed in his intention of introducing gemstones to all the readers, awakening in them an appreciation of the countless wonders of nature, and perhaps even a certain happy enchantment with, and love for, these aristrocratic foundlings.

Like mysterious flowering forces, crystals germinate in rocks still extant today, and their highest perfection, gemstones, which are formed through the interplay of mighty natural forces millions of years ago, inspire us with amazement and a curious awe. Thus, it is hardly surprising that, even in mankind's earliest history, colored pebbles, polished by the waves of the sea, were collected as "gemstones." The first intaglios and seal rings have come down to us from the ancient cultures of the Sumerians, Babylonians, and Egyptians. In those pre-Christian times men began decorating themselves with precious jewels, instead of with huge lions' manes, in order to attract women. Then, much later, such ornaments gradually became the perquisite of Eve's daughters, as an added attraction, as it were, to their feminine graces. But gemstones were also prized and sought after in ancient times as sacrificial gifts to the gods.

At the beginning of the fifth century St. Jerome discussed the relationship between the twelve gemstones in the breastplate of the Jewish High Priest of Jerusalem, the twelve months of the year, and the twelve signs of the zodiac. The phenomenon of the monthly and zodiacal stones seems, however, to have developed only after the eighteenth century in Poland, and the allocation of the stones has changed many times in the course of the centuries; recently, after the Second World War. In the Middle Ages—before it was understood how to cut them correctly—the flowers of the mineral kingdom became objects of deeply rooted symbolism in crowns and scepters. In Renaissance times man was first presumptuous enough to strip the crystalline symbols of their magic by cutting facets on them so as to reveal the mysteries dwelling within them. From the viewpoint of the twentieth century, freed from superstition as evidence of modern man's scientific knowledge, gemstones constitute the greatest investment in the smallest space. But today a mineral is raised to the royal status of a gemstone only when its dignity and value are derived from the three cardinal virtues: beauty, rarity, and durability.

1 Light kindles the glittering luster of gemstones, wakens their splendid colors, and reveals their limpid transparency.

Beauty: The Soul of Gemstones

*H*UMAN feeling for beauty is an age-old phenomenon that we experience only in moments of blessed illumination. Wherever beauty is apparent to us—whether in one of Nature's creations or in a masterpiece from the hand of man—it arouses a feeling of comfort, delight, and admiration. Beauty is the symbol of the ubiquitous law of creation to which man spontaneously and immediately responds, without consciously comprehending it or being able to express it in words. Beauty rejoices the eye and heart and gives wings to the spirit; indeed, so deeply does it pervade the mind that it never reveals itself to sober reasoning.

The beauty of gemstones may display itself in completely different ways: through the clear transparency, colorlessness, and fire-scattering brilliance in a brilliant-cut diamond; the luxurious splendor of color in the precious stones ruby, sapphire, and emerald; the attractive limpidity of pastel-colored beryls; the dreamy somnolence of the many-colored tourmalines; the mysterious sheen of light on cat's-eyes and star stones; the play of color in opal and spectrolite; and no less in the fantastic patterns of many ornamental stones. In all these spellbinding manifestations of beauty, light plays the chief role. In spite of all our knowledge of its physical nature, it still remains in essence an unsolved riddle which fills us with awe.

In the kingdom of the elect, the chosen one stands out epitomizing the noblest attributes of light—the ice tear, the diamond. Even in its colorless state it is king without peer; it comes even closer to the ideal of a gemstone when color, too, is inherent, for the blazing beauty of diamond springs not so much from its almost proverbial absence of color and purity, but much more from its glittering brilliance, arising from the combination of its adamantine luster, its high refraction of light, its color-scattering fire, and its vivid sparkle. In colorless stones these factors are naturally more easily visible than in colored ones. The luster is produced by reflection of light from the polished surface. The fire is the play of prismatic colors which emerge from the brilliant-cut diamond by means of the splitting, or dispersion, of white light into its rainbow colors. The light reflected back from inside the stone reinforces the glistening brilliance. The strong intensity of all these brilliance factors is due to the high refraction of light which results from the slowing of the velocity of light in diamond.

2 Diamond presents itself not only as a colorless
precious stone but in all known colors too.

The Beauty of Colored Gems

C_{OLOR} is the most beautiful manifestation of light and one of the most striking features of the material world. It spices Nature as salt does food. After the gray monotone of winter, man's eyes rejoice in the fresh, sparkling abundance of spring color. Color expresses dynamism and energy; unasked, it brings us cheerful serenity and uplifted spirits. So, too, the love of precious stones depends to a great extent on their richness of color. Unearthed from the dark underworld into the light, the essentially modest crystals owe their sublime dignity and glorious beauty to color alone. The world of human conceptions is mainly a world of the eye and thus a world of light and color. Its liveliness and its constantly changing play of light not only satisfy a general feeling for beauty; they are, rather, a functional need of mankind. Thus it is no chance that the striking colors of the three most precious stones—ruby, sapphire, and emerald—are generally felt to be the most pleasing and the most satisfying of all. This delightful impression on our eyes is certainly a very prosaic explanation of our longing for beauty. But perhaps the yearning desire for color may be less factually explained? Could not their power of attraction be based on this: that when we look at a glorious deep-colored stone we simply forget our conscious selves?—that we sink completely into dimly discerned depths?—that doors open to us which otherwise remain closed?—that pictures full of peace and bliss shape themselves before our inner eyes? We see indescribable landscapes of deep surging blue in the sapphire, veiled and unfathomable; explosions of light, consuming fires in the red glow of the ruby; leaping mountain streams, foaming seas, or peaceful gardens in the green of the emerald. Far from the glittering thrones of these high majesties, fascination and delight may also be experienced in the more modest gemstones. Thus, in the ultramarine blue of lapis lazuli we may imagine a piece of the starry heavens, opal conjures up the illusion of a merry harlequin, spectrolite captures in our hands a shimmering rainbow. Would not man's fantasy become impoverished without color? A liberating and yet restricting wonder about these mysterious connections starts to overwhelm us. In the next chapter, may our minds stay clear enough to grasp the bewildering mutual relationships in this outcome of breathtaking elective affinities in the origin of color.

3 The wealth of gemstone colors finds its richest
expression in the countless hues of the beryls.

The Cause of Colors

*H*ERE lightly brushed in and with variegated play, there firmly laid on or, as it were, solidified—the colors of gemstones manifest themselves in crystalline clarity and total beauty. The investigation and explanation of gem colors forms one of the most exciting chapters of gemmology. Optics and chemistry mesh in with the highly topical science of atomic structure and forces.

In technical language a distinction is made between self- or inherently-colored (idiochromatic) minerals and foreign or extraneously-colored (allochromatic) minerals. In the idiochromatic ones the pigmenting element is a constituent part of the chemical structure and thus an inherent (integral) component. Such gemstones as almandine, peridot, spessartite, malachite, rhodochrosite, rhodonite, and turquoise occur only in one single color and are fairly color-constant. The chemical composition of the allochromatic stones, on the other hand, when pure, produces completely colorless specimens. Whence comes their color, then? Eight chemical elements—titanium, chromium, iron, nickel, vanadium, manganese, cobalt, and copper—are characterized by an anomalous atomic structure. They cause the absolutely astonishing display of colors by their "accidental yet arbitrary presence." These chromophorous (color-imparting) foreign substances crept into the mineral as dust-fine metallic clouds, but are so sparsely distributed that they can only be traced by the spectroscope, their average order of magnitude amounting to no more than 1–5 percent by weight. Think of it! 1–5 percent is sufficient to convert worthless into precious! The majority of well-known gemstones are thus "invaded." Moreover, depending on the host structure, one given coloring agent can provoke different colors, for example, chromium can produce ruby, spinel red, emerald, and demantoid green.

The incorporation of these foreign elements, which distort the host structure, produces electromagnetic fields of tension with free energies in the crystal lattice. Light, in its turn, is likewise a form of electromagnetic energy, that is, the sum of variously high energies. A given energy charge corresponds to a definite wavelength, which affects our eyes as color. The light falling on a colored gemstone suffers a loss of a certain energy component at the color centers, i.e., a selective absorption takes place. Now, only that mixture of colors which has not been absorbed emerges from the gemstone. In ruby the entire green component and the greater part of the blue component of light is absorbed, so that only a mixture of red, yellow, and a very little blue can emerge. These colors together produce the beautiful carmine red of ruby.

4 The well-known colorless rock crystal has many colored brothers.

The Beauty of Phenomenal Stones

WITH the crystal-clear beauty of the chemically produced colors, we have still not reached the end of the chain of wonders, so incredible to the layman. However bewildering the almost inexhaustible variety of colors, yet more bewildering are the twinkling light displays of the phenomenal stones—of cat's-eyes and star stones, of moonstone, opal, and spectrolite. They exert less of a general attraction but an all the more distinctive beauty appealing to personal taste. Gemstone lore and superstition could scarcely find anywhere more fruitful soil than in these intangible visions reflected from the unplumbable depths of the stones' interiors or apparently sweeping over their surfaces. For the uninitiated, these visions are wreathed with inexplicable mysteries, but in actual fact they originate from purely optical properties of light rendered visible by structural peculiarities of the gemstones concerned.

Chatoyancy, or the cat's-eye effect, results from reflections of light from microscopically fine fibers or hollow channels, lying parallel to one another and traversing the entire body of the stone. If a domed surface curves above them, the light shrinks into a narrow line. Well-known examples are the golden-brown tiger's-eye, the blue falcon's-eye, and especially the most valuable of all, the bamboo-green to honey-colored chrysoberyl cat's-eye. Asterism, or star formation, is in fact merely a multiplication of the single chatoyancy, in which two or three rays of light cross one another and thus make up four- or six-rayed stars. The cause lies in the two or three systems of extremely fine, parallel fibers or minute needles which intersect at 90 degrees or 120 degrees. Star rubies and star sapphires exhibit this phenomenon at its most effective with six-rayed stars. There are, however, star spinels and star garnets too, displaying four- and six-rayed stars alternately.

Adularescence is the name given to the pale blue, surging shimmer of light which glides over the convex surface of a moonstone. It originates from interference of light when it strikes the fine lamellar structure of this gemstone. Interference is likewise responsible for the blue gleam of common labradorite.

Diffraction of light by the gratinglike packing of the spheres of which opal is composed causes its exquisite, color-flecked play of flames. The phenomenon is comparable with the colored image of a street lamp seen through the weave of an open umbrella.

5 The play of color of black opal scatters all the colors of the spectrum.

The Beauty of Ornamental Stones

THE beauty of translucent and opaque ornamental stones is of a capricious kind, since it must emerge without the favorable combination of transparency, brilliance, and fire. While the popularity of gemstones is explained by their luminous splendor of color or varying light effects, the enchantment of ornamental stones lies in their captivating appearance and the extraordinary individuality of their patterns.

In the phenomenal stones the inclusions are only slightly noticeable beneath the shimmering light effects; but in many ornamental stones, especially in agates, they are apparent in macroscopic sizes, that is, easily visible to the eye, and indeed frequently offer a feast for the eyes. They are primarily mineral inclusions whose origin is more recent than that of the ornamental stone embracing them. Mostly as iron or manganese solutions, they have forced their way from outside into cracks and fractures and, as the solution dried out, have crystallized there into the hydrous oxides of iron (brown iron) and manganese (psilomelanite and pyrolusite). Growth usually took place so rapidly that only dendritic or other fantastic skeletal crystals could develop. In this manner the coveted dendritic, mocha, and landscape agates originated. Dreamlike designs of inimitable grace and surprising regularity, illusions of landscapes, and hair-fine webs provide a fascination which arouses a painful collecting mania in the hearts of connoisseurs.

The temptation of contemplative lingering is obvious. The enchanted observer, letting his thoughts ramble enjoyably, is always expecting to discover ever new wonders, ever other pictures. The master painter Nature shows her most lavish side in the ornamental stones: many-streamered sheaves of fireworks explode, a mirage of fairy palaces and rolling hills shimmers on the horizon, primeval plants appear transfixed forever in stone, seismograph styluses draw trembling curves . . . and the best of it is that Nature has not preordained the designs but has sketched them from her own imagination and without models.

Thus each ornamental stone is resplendent in its own individual color, emphasized by the character of the graceful design: whether the green-banded malachite; or rhodochrosite with its pink-colored, blossomlike pattern; or turquoise, shot through with velvety brown matrix veins, or the gold-sprinkled lapis lazuli—the beauty of each and every one is incomparable.

6 Landscape agates tantalize the imagination with patterns suggesting fantastic panoramas.

Ennobling Rarity

THE subject of the rarity of gemstones, which so much enhances their prestige and value, leads us down into the dark, inaccessible depths of the earth's interior—to the birthplaces of the gemstones—where they were formed under the exertion of enormous natural forces. It was primarily there that the conditions critical for beauty, rarity, and durability were fulfilled; but it is strange and surprising that the majority of these most beautiful and valuable creations, conceived in the earth's womb, are composed of the most ordinary materials; namely, carbon (C), alumina (aluminium oxide, Al_2O_3), silica (silicon dioxide, SiO_2), lime (calcium carbonate, $CaCO_3$), and others besides. Considering the worldwide distribution of these common substances, it is remarkable that gemstones are so rare. Apart from the requirement that, in the first place, factors promoting crystallization must be present, in many gemstones of simple composition it is the extremely rare coloring agent (e.g., chromium in alexandrite, ruby, and emerald) that determines the distinct rarity; in gemstones of complex composition, on the other hand, rarity is occasioned by an important but minimally represented constituent such as fluorine in topaz and boron in tourmaline. Many a mineral formation is virtually unique, as in the case of benitoite, because the participating chemical elements were present only once, and in a single locality of the earth, at the same time so as to combine in the correct stoichiometric proportions for the mineral concerned.

By far the majority of gemstones have grown as crystals. This means that they consist of ordered matter, in which the structural elements—that is, the atoms—are arranged according to rigorous laws. Of two adjacent atoms, one is always positively, the other negatively charged. These oppositely charged atoms, named ions, attract each other. The force holding them together is called cohesion and determines the solidity of the crystal. Under favorable conditions in melts, solutions, and gases, ions which are oppositely charged and complementary to one another may be found together; they form up in lines, construct planes, and build themselves into space-filling crystal lattices, arranged in accordance with definite laws, their inner structure being revealed on the outside by an architecture of many faces.

In connection with the rarity of gemstones, the question now arises: under what conditions of mineral formation can specially beautiful and large crystals originate? Geology teaches us that the great developmental processes which the crust of our earth has undergone in the course of its history have led to the formation of mineral deposits under

7 Hydrothermally produced emerald prisms on a mother
rock of contact metamorphosed limestone. Colombia.

8 Typical example of pneumatolytic-hydrothermal formation: yellow-brown topaz grown on a rock crystal.

extremely varied conditions. They are governed by a twofold event, whose phases are closely related to one another: the formation of mountains and the uprise of molten masses, so-called magmas (from the Greek *magis,* kneaded masses), from the interior of the earth. An extensive zone of such molten matter, which on account of its chemical composition (*silica* and *ma*gnesium) is designated sima, spreads beneath the crust of the earth. The molten masses of the sima in the depths of the earth are inaccessible to us. Incontrovertible proof of its presence is provided by observations of the propagation of earthquake waves and naturally by the basaltic lava flows of volcanoes. From this subterranean sima diamond originates as an early crystallization and reaches the earth's surface by way of volcanic chimneys which break through it. Of similar origin is pyrope. Some of the Siam and Australian sapphires and many zircons also occur in basaltic lava flows from the sima.

The spherical shell of the sima is enclosed on the outside by the solid crust of rocks, the lithosphere. Into the latter, melts from the region of magmatic rocks are forced during mountain building; their composition is characterized by a combination of *silica* and *alumina*, whence the material is named sial. These sialic melts bring us a much greater number of gemstones in their cooling products—the rocks and mineral deposits of the earth's surface resulting from solidification through cooling.

The congealing of a magma into rock through crystallization is a very complicated process which has taken place over millions of years in three great cycles, namely, the magmatic, the metamorphic, and the sedimentary cycles. Within the *magmatic cycle* the sialic magmas have, during their crystallization, gone through a series of stages which are subdivided according to their sequence and cooling temperatures into the *liquid-magmatic* (1500–700°C.), pegmatitic (700–500°C.), pneumatolytic (500–400°C.), and hydrothermal (400–100°C.) phases. In the *liquid-magmatic* phase the main crystallization took place in the molten zone while the definitive formation of the plutonic rocks was going on; examples of such rocks are granites, diorites, and gabbros. Thereby, according to the composition of the magma, the most important rock-forming minerals, such as mica, feldspar, quartz, olivine, and others, were segregated out in orderly succession. The gemstone labradorite, with its variety spectrolite, as well as peridot and some zircons are likewise rock-forming minerals of this phase. The medley of accessory gemstones crystallizing out, such as apatite, beryl, spinel, tourmaline, and others, were still at this stage unimportant owing to their microscopically small size.

As the crystallization process of the liquid-magmatic phase proceeded the magmatic melts became more and more exhausted, leaving behind residual melts, in which the so-called volatile constituents of the magma, such as water, boron, chlorine, fluorine, carbonic acid, phosphorus, sulphur, uranium, zirconium, and so on, then precious and heavy metals, as well as a whole series of rare elements, were meanwhile concentrated by differentiation. Here, too, silica and alumina still played a decisive role. The internal pressure of these superheated melt solutions was very high, and the volatile residual substances gushing copiously out of the cooling magmas raised it even higher. Thus these residual melts emerged from the realm of the plutonic rocks under high pressure and forced their way along cracks and fissures—so-called gangues—into the adjacent country rocks, where their chemical and thermal action produced great changes. The most important of these veinrocks are the pegmatites (from the Greek *pegma* = texture or framework), and the processes peculiar to them formed the *pegmatitic* phase. In it numerous coarsely crystalline silicate minerals were segregated and precipitation of quartz and feldspar took place. The great majority of pegmatites are related to granite and similar acid (that is, silica-rich) plutonic rocks; basic (that is, silica-poor) magmas do not give rise to pegmatites. The pegmatitic minerals crystallizing out from hot, watery residual fluids found specially favorable growth conditions. The content of volatile constituents made these pegmatitic melts not only very fluid and mobile so that large crystals could grow in them, but also chemically very active, too. Despite the paucity of nucleation sites they were astonishingly eager to form crystals; for the chemically active mixtures stimulated crystal growth, as so-called mineralizers. Thus the crystals attained the requisite purity and size for gemstones. The widespread fairly large druses in many pegmatite districts are well-known as storehouses of exceptionally beautiful crystals. For the zone of pegmatite formation is also the home of the largest crystals known in the solid crust of the earth, and thus at the same time the most important nursery of gemstones; for example, it produces apatite, beryl, chrysoberyl, euclase, fluorite, kunzite, moonstone, sapphire, topaz, tourmaline (black), and again some of the zircons, and many other somewhat less significant gemstones.

As a result of further cooling of the postmagmatic residual melts the volatile constituents became even more strongly enriched, and there arose gaseous and particularly hydrous solutions, from which developed the *pneumatolytic* deposits (Greek *pneuma* = breath; French *lyein* = to loose). The extremely reaction-prone pneumatolytic mineral solutions were able to force their way, even more strongly than the pegmatitic ones, into limestones, dolomites, and clays and to act upon them, as they are very easily chemically attacked. Through the strong chemical activity of the volatile substances, a brisk exchange of materials took place, which led to alteration of the adjacent country rocks, so-called contact metamorphism, from which quite new minerals and rocks—contact minerals and contact rocks—were produced. In this manner deposits were formed, which have become world renowned for their amazingly varied mineral associations (parageneses, from the Greek *para* = near, beside, and *genesis* = origin) and beautifully developed crystals, for example, those of Ceylon, of Mogok in Burma, and in the Urals.

Offspring of the pneumatolytic phase are ruby, sapphire, and spinel in contact metamorphosed limestone, with zircon as their companion (Burma and, in part, Ceylon); emerald in metamorphic schists (Rhodesia, Transvaal), and, together with alexandrite, in contact metamorphosed biotite schists (Urals), lapis lazuli in contact metamorphosed limestones (Afghanistan and Chile), and so on.

The *hydrothermal* phase (Greek *hydor* = water, *thermos* = hot) formed the close of the magmatic cycle; in its course hot, watery mineral solutions rose up from the depths into clefts and porous zones of the rocks and penetrated, according to the available space, into fine veins or massive lodes. From these hydrothermal solutions, which carried mainly silica, as well as residual constituents of the rock-forming chemical elements and heavy metals, the dissolved substances crystallized out through cooling and formed vein fillings. To these, in addition to fluorite, belong chiefly the varieties of the quartz group: amethyst, rock crystal, smoky quartz, and citrine, as well as precious tourmaline and also, in part,

9 Quartz druse lined with violet amethyst terminations.

topaz. Of hydrothermal origin, too, is the emerald found in calcareous shales at Muzo, Colombia. Hydrothermal mineral parageneses are the most important precipitators of gold, silver, copper, tin, zinc, uranium, and many other heavy metals, and are on that account of special economic value. Between the individual phases of the magmatic cycle additional multiple transitions are known.

A further important rock-forming process was the *metamorphic* cycle, which included the large group of the crystalline schists. They originated from already existing magmatic or sedimentary rocks which, bedded in the earth's crust, did not remain unaltered, but, under the influence of increased pressure, and access of heat and circulating solutions, suffered a recrystallization (metamorphism). These metamorphic processes were mostly associated with the uprise of magmatic melts or with mountain-building forces, whose often unilateral pressure imparted a slatelike structure to the resultant rocks. Among the metamorphic rocks belong such well-known ones as the gneisses, mica schists, serpentines, and marbles. Among the gemstones, they offer us only almandine— frequently found as an accessory mineral in gneisses and mica schists—as well as both the jade minerals, jadeite and nephrite. Certainly in the last two, additional contact metamorphism of sialic magmas has also been in play.

The *cycle of weathering processes,* which in itself contributes only unattractive rocks and minerals, is poor in gemstones. There are only four gems which are weathering products, namely, turquoise, chrysoprase, malachite, and azurite. Turquoise is a by-product of the weathering of acid magmatic rocks in conjunction with the deposition of copper ores nearby. Its formation derives from circulating meteoric waters and is promoted by the continuing attrition of the rock by hot water solutions. Thereby alumina was released from the feldspar of the magmatic rock, while phosphoric acid was set free from the apatite. The color-active copper originated from the copper ores which were interbedded in the rock. Chrysoprase is the end-product of a complicated chain of unique altering and concentrating processes, in which nickel-bearing basic rocks were involved. At the end of these processes chrysoprase developed in lodes and cavities of the weathered masses as a new deposit in the form of a finely fibrous quartz, between whose fibers nickel grains were embedded, giving it its apple-green color. Green malachite and blue azurite resulted from surface weathering of copper ores under the action of water and carbonic acid.

The occurrences emerging from all the processes of formation described above and responsible for the rarity of gemstones constitute the actual birthplaces, that is to say, the primary deposits of gemstones.

In the weathered debris which accumulated from the erosion of rocks, gemstones —resistant to attack by weathering factors—lie well preserved, and can be recovered easily by washing. This kind of deposit is called "eluvial drift," and gemstones are often strongly concentrated in it.

The *sedimentary* and last rock-forming cycle is not of any importance in the formation of gemstone deposits. In it, after the weathering of rocks had taken place, loose strata were formed, such as gravels, sands, and clays, deposited from water and air, which in time consolidated into conglomerates, sandstones, and shales. The rhodochrosite stalagmites near San Luis in Argentina constitute a young formation of the sedimentary cycle. The sedimentary detritus and accumulations are, however, precisely those from which the majority of gemstones are won. They did not, of course, originate within them, but were amassed in the weathered sediments, by water transport. Thus gemstones here no longer constitute primary deposits, but secondary ones. During their transport by water a sorting corresponding to their specific gravity took place, in that the heavier (higher specific gravity) gemstones sank and collected in hollows, or so-called pockets. As this accumulation took place by water, and likewise a natural puddling occurred, these secondary occurrences are often called placer deposits or alluvial gem gravels. Such gravels are found both in present-day stream beds and valley bottoms as well as in the older river terraces and bank dunes deposited higher up. In this way Nature gives them to us in the truest sense as a gift; for through enrichment in the detritus, a natural selection of the best qualities has occurred, and, moreover, mining can be operated at considerably reduced cost.

In the world map of gemstone deposits one is struck by their restriction to, or rather, their concentration in the zones near the equator. Obviously this can only signify that formations of the gem-rich phases of the sial cropped out particularly abundantly in these districts. In the course of world history the intensity and dimensions of sialic magma uprisings in conjunction with mountain-building have consistently decreased. Our young fold mountains—the Alps, the Andes, the Himalayas—which rose in the Tertiary era only—contain far fewer magmatic rocks and postmagmatic derivates, e.g. pegmatites, than the old mountain stumps of the former massive primeval continents of the earth. Of these, the hypothetical continent Gondwanaland corresponds with the regions most prolific in gems, for remnants of it form the basement of South America, Africa, Madagascar, Southeast Asia, Borneo and Australia, where valuable gemstones are chiefly found. North America lies on a continental shield which geologists have named Laurentia. By far the greater northern part of it, however, is overlain by deposits of the Ice Age, so that this subsurface is not accessible to us.

Durability: The Third Main Attribute of Gemstones

GEMSTONES are surrounded by an awe-inspiring ambience of far distant birth and age-long past. They are timeless and never age; to them alone perpetual youth is granted. When we human beings are long dead and gone, gemstones will still be here to rejoice our descendants with their sparkle and fire. Man—who has hardly discovered any other means of preserving his memory unforgotten for posterity—recognizes in a gemstone the legendary symbol of permanence. Thus the third prerequisite necessary for these illustrious jewels is fulfilled: survival. A survival in inviolable beauty!

This enviable attribute is imparted to gemstones by their crystalline solidity, their great hardness, their inflexible resistance to chemical attack, and the color-fading action of light. They are thus proof against harmful environmental influences which might alter their luster, color, or form. The distinguishing characteristic of hardness protects them from outer damage such as scratches, chafing, and corrosion. Among their peers, they certainly recognize a respectable succession of rank, which was set out in 1812 by the mineralogist Friedrich Mohs and is called, after him, the Mohs hardness scale. Its very general function signifies that each higher gemstone is able to scratch the lower ones. The ten hardness stages are represented by talc (1), gypsum (2), calcite (3), fluorite (4), apatite (5), feldspar (6), quartz (7), topaz (8), corundum (9), and diamond (10). Hardness is thus a diagnostic property of each stone. It is indirectly related to the chemical structure and directly dependent on the regular arrangement of the atoms. The latter determines the strength of the inner bonding forces (cohesion) and the degree of hardness. In diamond the bond between neighboring identical carbon atoms is extraordinarily strong, and the space packing the tightest possible. Therein lies the reason for the unusually high refractive index and the unsurpassed hardness of this precious stone.

It seems almost insolence that man, with his skill, should dare to attack the extreme hardness of gemstones by giving the rough plain pebbles a facet-rich appearance by cutting, thus waking the slumbering beauty within them to glistening intensity. The art of cutting colored stones, amongst which all gemstones except diamond and agate are included, requires much experience and a high consciousness of responsibility; for it is indeed costly material that must be enhanced. Most rough stones, because of their size or unsuitable form, must first be cut up. For this a metallic circular saw is used, whose edge is

22

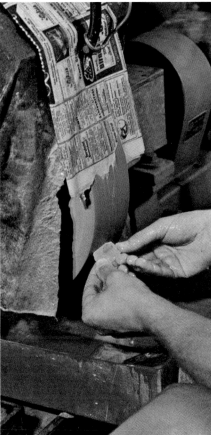

10 The large gemstones are cut up on the circular saw.

11 On the grinding wheel the gems are ground into a rough, preliminary shape.

12 On the faceting lap the gems are faceted and polished.

impregnated with diamond dust. The second process, the grinding, shapes the crude preform chosen after evaluating the rough stone and planning the cut. This is done on a carborundum grinding wheel. After this, the roughly ground stone is cemented on to a dop stick, whose other end is pointed so that during cutting and polishing it can be fitted into the jamb peg. The last and most subtle process is carried out on a faceting lap. The gem stick holding the stone is supported by a jamb peg and set in the correct position by the cutter. Each of the individual angle positions corresponding to the series of facets is selected by fitting the gem stick into the various holes of the jamb peg. Finally, polishing follows on the polishing lap, which is built exactly as is the faceting lap but is provided with a considerably finer abrasive. In cutting and polishing, each gemstone is individually treated, in that the material of the lap, as well as the cutting and polishing powders, must be suited to its cohesion properties. Cutting of gemstones is craft and art at the same time. It requires, above all, an ability to sense the nature of the stone, in order to shape it according to its character and endow it with shining beauty.

Diamond: King of Precious Stones

I N its dazzling beauty and the unchanging stability of its value diamond is among the best known, most beloved, and most coveted precious stones of the earth. In many respects it is the most unusual and most interesting mineral within the world of matter known to us. It is unique and attractive not only as a most costly gemstone or as the hardest of all minerals—and thus the most valuable material of modern technology—but above all as the most important evidence for the constitutional and environmental conditions at the time of its evolution in the depths of the earth, which are completely inaccessible to us and will remain so for a long time to come. There Nature endowed the diamond with the preeminent properties of a precious stone.

Diamond! What a magic power this name has! Diamonds are symbols of brilliance, ornaments of crowns and consecrated vessels, heart's desire, and adornment of queens—diamonds have for centuries been the sum total of highest value, sublimest beauty. With diamonds are closely bound the fates of rulers and adventurers, the fortunes of peoples, families and individuals. Diamond is the precious stone which fills the starry hours of our lives with its light and forever more recalls them to us—birth, engagement, marriage, first child, jubilees, and so on. Unmarred clarity, wonderful purity combined with its fascinating sparkle and scatter of rainbow-colored fire, as well as vivid brilliance, raise it by right to be "king of precious stones." But what is it, this most mysterious, most famous and most glittering of all gemstones? Whence does it come? How does it originate, how is it found? How is it perfected? What adventures has it had? All these and other questions will now be briefly answered.

The ancient Greeks spoke of the diamond as *adamas*—the steel-hard and invincible one. From this came the medieval words *ademant, demant,* and finally *diamond.* Even six hundred years before Christ, it was known to ancient man from India, where diamonds were washed out from the river gravels. All the important Indian occurrences extend along the eastern side of the Deccan Plateau. In general they may be divided into the following main fields: Golconda, with the most important finds along the Pennar and Kistna rivers; the Brahmani and Mahanadi group with alluvial mining in the rivers of the same names; the Panna group with two small primary occurrences as outcropping "pipes." Occasionally Indian diamonds are found in loose river detritus. Much more important, however, are the accumulations in higher river terraces and sediments in which the diamonds lie as a secondary deposit interbedded with conglomerates and sandstones. From

24

13 Rough and cut diamonds in various colors
and forms, unset and made up into jewelry.

time immemorial the weight of this "earth fruit"—as the Indians took it to be—has been measured on a simple balance against the seeds of the carob tree, which are called *cattie*. Our word carat, the unit of weight of 0.2 gm., comes from the Arabic *qīrāt* and the Greek *keration,* which referred to the pod of the locust tree.

If the awe-inspiring miracle of this peerless gemstone is overwhelming, the adventures that some of the famous diamonds took are enthralling. Most of them originated in India. Thus, the legendary Hope, a blue diamond of 44.5 carats, believed to be identical with the Blue Tavernier, reached the court of Louis XIV in 1668. After it had been stolen during the French Revolution and probably recut to prevent recognition, it was acquired by the English banker and art lover Henry Thomas Hope. Its restless wanderings ended in 1958 when the New York diamond merchant Harry Winston gave it to the Smithsonian Institution. Also of Indian origin is the "Mountain of Light" or Koh-i-noor, which must once have weighed 700 carats. Its history can be traced back to the fourteenth century, when it belonged to the family of the Rajahs of Malwa. Wars accompanied its way to the Peacock Throne of the Great Mogul; intrigue delivered it into the hands of Nadir Shah. When the Persian conqueror invited his former adversary to a banquet, he tricked him into the customary gesture of friendship in the Orient—the exchange of turbans—knowing full well, from the spying of a slave girl, that the coveted gem was hidden in the folds of the latter's headdress. Later, after its return to India, the East India Company presented it in 1850 to Queen Victoria. Under her orders it was recut, the work taking thirty-eight days and its weight being reduced to 108 carats. As one of the most valuable diamonds the world has ever seen, it now decorates the Queen Mother's crown. The Orloff, weighing almost 200 carats, was one of the eyes of the Hindu god Sri-Ranga before it was stolen from a temple in Mysore in southern India, by a French soldier clad as a monk. The Russian Count Alexei Grigorievich Orloff purchased it in 1774 from Amsterdam, in order to honor Catherine the Great with it. The rose-cut stone, which is outstanding for its extraordinary clarity, was then mounted at the tip of the Russian scepter.

The Indian occurrences, exploited over thousands of years, gradually became exhausted. Then, suddenly in the year 1728, just at the right moment, the first Brazilian diamonds appeared in Lisbon; since 1721 the gold panners of Brazil had used these glittering stones as counters, never dreaming that they were far more valuable than the scarce gold which they, with daily toil, were washing out of the rivers. After news of the diamond find became known a very active search began in all the rivers, and—lo! the effort was not in vain: every river yielded diamonds. At first, to be sure, the European market bristled distrustfully against the new Brazilian diamonds. It was asserted that they were too hard to be cut, or that they were far less valuable stones. Only when the Brazilians smuggled their diamonds into India through the port of Goa did the latter find entry, through the trading centers there, into Europe. The Star of the South, a diamond

14 Crater of a so-called pipe mine in South Africa, mined by open cast methods.

with an uncut weight of more than 260 carats, brought a Brazilian slave girl, who discovered it in 1853, freedom and a lifelong income. In 1938 the President Vargas, weighing nearly 600 carats, was found in the São Antonio River and was cut by Harry Winston into twenty-nine smaller gem diamonds.

Through the discoveries in Africa the diamond trade took a mighty upswing. The find by a farmer's boy, Erasmus Stephanus Jacobs, was confirmed by the Cape Town mineralogist, Dr. W. G. Atherstone, in 1866 as the first genuine African diamond. One year later, at the world exhibition in Paris, under the name of the Eureka, it aroused enormous interest and simultaneously lit the fuse of the first African diamond rush. It was hardly blessed with luck, however, for not until 1869 was another large diamond found—the 83.5-carat Star of Africa—this time in the neighborhood of the Orange River, by a Griqua shepherd boy. The district in question was soon almost overflowing with adventurers fired by diamond fever. On the smallest pegged-out plot, everyone for himself and cheek by jowl with each other, they dug at first in the red lateritic soil, but later, with more accurate knowledge, in the deeper lying "blue ground." Often the price for a

27

15 Primitive mining by diggers on the placer fields of the Vaal River in South Africa.

diamond was paid with a life, through the collapse of undermined shafts. In order to clear up this chaos, prevent mine accidents and strife between employers and diggers, and guard against market crises, the Englishman Cecil John Rhodes, with support from wealthy undertakings—chiefly the Rothschild Bank—gradually bought up the farmland of the De Beers and the Kimberley mines. In 1888 he was able to enter De Beers Consolidated Mines, Ltd. in the Kimberley trade register. Since then the production and sale of diamonds have been supervised by this monopolistic cartel. The most prolific diamond mines of South Africa have been the De Beers, the Kimberley, the Wesselton, the Dutoitspan, and the Bultfontein. The Jagersfontein rates as the queen of the South African mines, while the Premier is the largest diamond mine in the world. It produced, in 1905, the largest of all diamonds, the giant Cullinan of 3,106 carats. This was later cut into nine large and ninety-six smaller gem diamonds. The first diamond deposit systematically sought, and found by accurate geological methods, was the very rich occurrence near Mwadui in Tanzania, which contains large quantities of the finest gem diamonds. From it came the 54-carat Elizabeth II diamond, a pink gem of great rarity, which its finder and owner, Dr. J. T. Williamson, presented to the future Queen Elizabeth II of Great Britain. New discoveries are constantly being made, as for instance that of the very important Finsch mine near Kimberley in 1965, and the huge Orapa mine in Botswana.

In the Soviet Union the first diamond placers worth mining were revealed in 1949 on the central Siberian Plateau, which lies in Yakutia between the Lena and Yenisei rivers. A few years later, in 1954, the young mineralogist L. Popugaeva, while following garnet gravel, stumbled on a diamond-bearing kimberlite pipe, which she named Sarzina. Other mines opened up since then are the Mir, the Udatschnaya, and the Aichal. Their gangue material consists of kimberlite which, despite its many varieties, resembles the basaltic kimberlites of South Africa. The Siberian "pipes" yield mainly industrial diamonds in ideal sizes; but just recently very large gem diamonds have also come from them; in 1967 the Maria diamond of 106 carats, in 1968 the Stalingrad, which weighed 166 carats, and, shortly afterward, from the same mine near Mirny, a 236-carat diamond.

Although diamond is not only the gemstone best known to the layman but equally the most intensively investigated mineral, it nevertheless continues to pose scientists more puzzles than any other substance. But never, not even in the face of their sober and factual findings, does it lose a jot of its magic. On the contrary, through precise examination of the material the true miracle of its nature was first unfolded. Diamond is the only precious stone which consists of a single element, namely quadrivalent carbon (C). It differs from common graphite and coal only in the extraordinarily close cubic space packing of the C atoms, which, together with the strong cohesion of its bonds, is responsible for its unequalled hardness (which, at 10, occupies the top place on the Mohs hardness scale); and in the surpassing refraction of light, whence its dazzling brilliance and strong dispersive power originate. Because of the relative lightness of carbon, its specific gravity amounts only to 3.52. The form of the unit cell of diamond, which crystallizes in the cubic system, produces a tetrahedron (a body bounded by four triangular faces). The commonest growth habits are the octahedron (bounded by eight triangular faces), the cube, and the rhomb-dodecahedron (bounded by twelve rhomb-shaped faces). The cutting industry noticed long ago that misshapen diamond crystals can be cleaved more easily and better than well-formed to perfectly formed ones; however, it was reserved to scientific research to recognize that a distinguishable state of the included trace elements was the cause of this ambivalent behavior. These elements were ascertained to be responsible for the colors and other optical and electronic properties of diamond, on account of which it has become a material with many uses in modern technology. The most widespread trace element is nitrogen. It is found in all diamonds of Type I, while those of Type II have none. These two structurally distinct diamond types fall again, in their turn, into two subclasses. In diamonds of Type Ia, in which the proportion of nitrogen to carbon is high (1:1,000), the nitrogen atoms unite in groups of minute platelets. Such diamonds are colorless. In diamonds of Type Ib the nitrogen atoms are built into the diamond structure as substitutions in disperse (finely distributed) form and give rise, according to their quantity, to the brown, yellow (as in the Florentine and the Tiffany), and green (for example, the Dresden Green) colors. All diamonds of Type I are characterized by good, well-developed crystal forms and poor cleavage. The nitrogen-free Type II diamonds give themselves away externally by their misshapen forms, on which hardly a single crystal face can be recognized, and by their easy cleavage.

Type IIa provides the purest diamonds, which contain no nitrogen and thus are completely colorless. When manganese is present as a trace element a rose-pink color results (as in the Regent and the Williamson). Type IIb is characterized by slight traces of aluminium, which not only colors such diamonds blue (like the Hope and the Wittelsbach), but also turns them into semiconductors which are vital to the electronic industry.

The structural build of diamonds arouses our curiosity about the conditions of their formation. The interpretation prevailing today rests on the hypothesis that in a very early era there existed above the sima widespread focal points of magma in which dense olivine aggregates gradually became concentrated. In a second, much later period, basic magma masses were forced, under immense internal pressure, into fracture zones of the middle and upper crust, and alteration of the olivine aggregates into eclogite knolls came about. These consist of olivine, garnet, and diopside. In the course of this unusual metamorphism, which took place at about 25 kilometers depth under an overburden pressure of about 50,000 atmospheres and at temperatures of about 1,300° C., the formation of diamonds occurred at the same time as that of other minerals. In a third phase the diamonds were catapulted in sporadic explosive eruptions from the earth's interior to its surface and embedded in the kimberlite rock which formed as the lava masses cooled. In the course of the last two hundred million years the friable kimberlite crumbled away through the destructive ravages of weathering. The diamonds thus freed were in part set down in the detritus of river beds, and in part carried down to the sea coast and there deposited either in coastal sediments or in shoal banks in the ocean. As a result of this, the diamonds are won from very varying strata: from the primary rock fill of the volcanic necks (the "blue ground"), from the secondary gem gravels of the river beds, and from the marine beds of coastal sands. Consequently, very distinct mining methods have been developed, ranging from highly mechanized operations in South Africa, Tanzania, and Siberia, through the most primitive excavation methods of private diggers in all parts of the world, to the imposing array of machine installation and earth moving along the coast of southwest Africa. In contrast to the primary deposits, where some 3.6 tons produce one carat of diamond (1:18 million), the ratio of the littoral mining areas in southwest Africa amounts to only 1:80 million (i.e. one carat of diamond from sixteen tons of spoil). Of the world's annual production of diamonds, which in 1967 totalled 42.4 million carats, only approximately 21 percent, or 9 million carats, were diamonds of gem quality.

16 In the extensively mechanized production from marine deposits, the most modern machinery is employed to shift the huge quantities of sand.

Glassy and unattractive, shapeless and rough, diamonds can hardly be told from ordinary pebbles when, separated from their common brethren in their long treatment process, they at last arrive on the sorting table. Then man, with his knowledge and his skill, transforms them into objects of lustrous life. Giving them a facet-rich cut brings their beauty to scintillating fruition, displays their clear transparency, and sparks their high intensity of light—that unique combination of optical properties which is described as brilliance. Brilliance is created by the combined effects of adamantine luster (reflection of light from the polished surface), high refraction of light (diamond has a refractive index of 2.42, which means that light in diamond travels 2.42 times more slowly than in air), total reflection of the rays returned from the interior of the cut stone, dazzling fire of the light emerging from the stone dispersed into its component colors, and vivid sparkle. Diamond cutting is both science and art at one and the same time. The first stage is to establish the form by cleaving or, nowadays, principally by sawing on a very fine, circular metal saw. Depending on the size and the individual resistance, this can last hours or days. Before the two different sized parts can be cut into brilliants the cutter gives them a roughly circular form by rounding the pointed corners. For faceting and polishing, the rounded diamond, held in a dop, is lowered on to the quickly rotating cutting lap, which is coated with diamond powder and oil. During this most delicate phase of the cutting process the cutter sets down the diamond and lifts it up again hundreds of times in order to supervise his cut. But however carefully a diamond is cut, about half its weight is always lost in the process. Then, finally, after day- or week-long care, the diamond has become a brilliant-cut gem—a glittering jewel with its rich pattern of planes and geometrically shaped facets and the glistening play of light of its fiery brilliance. It is of unsurpassable beauty, arousing enraptured delight and astonished wonder.

Yet, however important the cutting is for the inimitable beauty of the brilliant-cut diamond, it is only one of the Four Cs, that is, carat, clarity, color, and cut, which together constitute the qualitative factors of the worth of a diamond. There is a widespread misconception among the public that a good diamond must be blue-white and flawlessly clear. Really blue-white diamonds are extremely rare, so rare indeed that many a diamond merchant has never encountered a blue-white diamond in his life. The subtle color nuances from blue-white through finest white, white, off-white, and yellowish to yellow apply only to the so-called white, i.e. colorless, group. The full-colored varieties are classed as fancy diamonds. As with the color, the same applies also to their clarity. Diamonds are precious marvels of Nature's creation and often carry within them clear evidence of their laborious birth, in the form of inclusions, which perhaps in the future will one day be seen as valuable proof of natural origin. Generally these involve diamond's twin brothers which were formed together with it: olivine, garnet, chrome spinel, diopside, enstatite, and many others—all are likewise gemstones which, in macroscopic size, are cut and highly esteemed by collectors. Diamonds in which an experienced expert can discover no inclusions with the help of tenfold magnification pass as internally flawless—the highest clarity grade of the trade. Thereafter follow several clarity grades down to stones full of inclusions, which mark the boundary between gem and industrial diamonds.

Depending on the original crystal form, various shapes of cut have been developed. The ideal cutting style is the round brilliant cut with 57 facets (1 table, 32 crown facets, and 24 pavilion facets). Often the point is truncated by the cullet, so that it does not get chipped. Favorite fancy cuts are the ship-shaped navette or marquise, the rodlike baguette, the trap cut, often called emerald-cut, and the drop form.

17 Sawing: Braced between two brass holders, so-called pots, the diamond crystal rests on the phosphor-bronze saw blade.

18 Bruting: Two diamonds are rubbed against one another in order to round them.

19 Faceting and Polishing: The diamond, mounted in a dop, is faceted and polished on the polishing wheel, called "skyf."

The "fragment of Eternity," as Indians call the diamond, has been from time immemorial the epitome of strength and courage. As the birthstone for April it is credited with freeing the spirit from anxieties, making poison ineffective, and its owner invincible, if—so the legend runs—his mind is lofty and his thoughts noble. Through its immaculate clarity it has embodied to the present day the highest of virtues and is considered a symbol of happiness. Above all goods and chattels mankind has prudently and carefully treasured its value as the most precious jewel as well as the very smallest form of dependable investment. Scientists have still, after all this time, not completely fathomed diamond: it remains wrapped in mystery and still provides them with many riddles for the future. For example, it has till now obstinately resisted all efforts to synthesize it in gem quality, and thus remains in this respect, too, *adamas*, the unconquerable.

So diamond displays, now as then, the majesty of Nature in radiant beauty and splendor, and its crystalline clarity and dazzling fire are a reflection and symbol of the sublime and timeless grandeur of creation.

The Colorful Corundum Family

THE sight of the glittering color splendor of the corundum family is enough to arouse in even the dullest spirit a bright enthusiasm. Like an alpine meadow in late springtime, these colored buds, crystallized by mineral husbandry, sprout in every imaginable shade of blue, yellow, and orange, in pink, green, violet, and brown. Some, seemingly still in bud and awaiting maturity, daydream in pale, muted tones; others, more striking, have been kissed awake by the sun and called into leaping life and glowing color. Moreover these colored blossoms from a charming May bouquet are of clearest transparency; as if washed clean by a sharp mountain wind. Their hues are pure and clearly definable. Thus yellow corundums shine out completely yellow, the red sparkle in purest red, the blue ones are resplendent with noblest blue, and the violet ones exactly match one's notion of the cardinals' color. At the baptism of this colorful family of precious stones, the godparents were the Sanskrit word *kuruwinda* and the Hindi word *kurund*. Among them are included the stones most highly prized for their beauty and rarity, namely, the red ruby and the blue sapphire. In contrast to ruby and sapphire, the colored fancy sapphires require the adjectival prefix of their color, thus yellow, green, or violet sapphire, likewise pink or purple sapphire, or even more correctly, yellow corundum, pink corundum, and so on.

The corundums are crystallized alumina, that is to say, they consist of a combination of aluminium and oxygen (Al_2O_3). Aluminium is renowned as a light metal and oxygen is a very light gas, and yet this combination produces a heavy, hard, and durable mineral. The regular arrangement of each aluminium atom above and below three oxygen atoms lying in a plane in the crystal lattice of corundum leads to the formation of a trigonal crystal architecture, which is expressed externally by a sixfold framework of faces. The form of sapphire is often governed by several six-sided double pyramids with or without intervening prisms. This combination of forms results in barrel-shaped crystals, which are particularly typical of Ceylon sapphires. Ruby mostly takes up a squat habit, which arises from the combination of short six-sided prisms with large basal faces, whose corners are truncated by small rhombohedral faces. The degree of hardness within the Mohs scale lies at 9, and yet its cutting hardness is some 140 times less than that of diamond, though about seven times higher than that of topaz which represents the next stage below it. The high specific gravity of 4 assists its recovery by means of the widely used washing process, in which corundum separates itself, by sinking, from lighter and

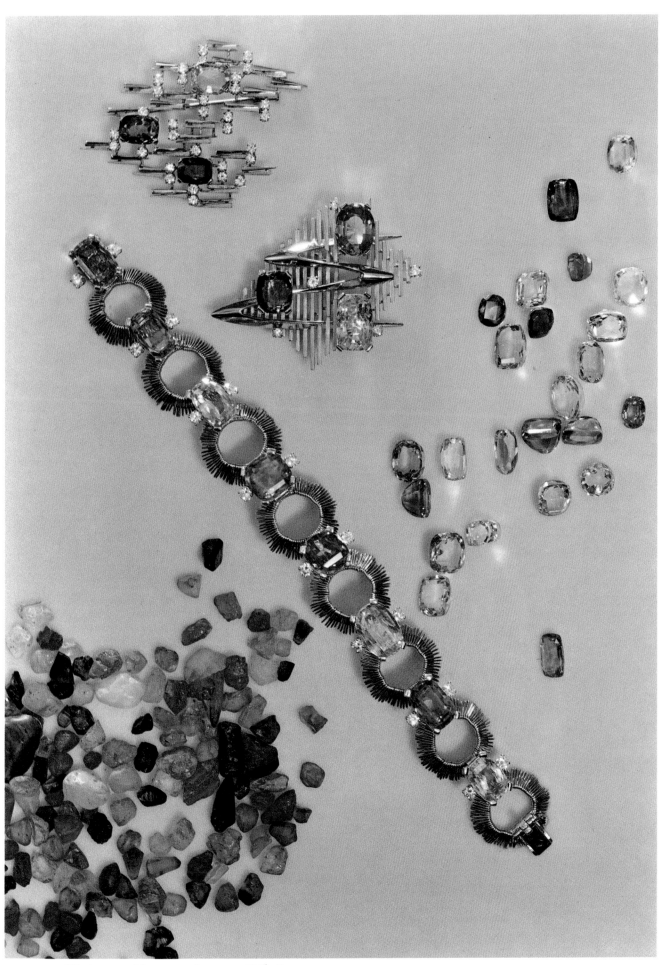

20 The beauty of the cut specimens would hardly
be suspected from the colored corundum pebbles.

21 Recovery of gemstones from the rivers of Ceylon is carried out by dredging with a long-handled rakelike scraper, locally called a *mamoti*.

often less valuable accompanying material. Corundum owes its beautiful high luster and vivid brilliance to its high refractive index, whose average lies at 1.765. Indeed, it is the purity of its colors and the vividness of its play of light that distinguishes corundum from members of other color-rich gemstones families.

Chemically pure, crystallized aluminium oxide (alumina/corundum) is completely colorless and more or less corresponds to the leucosapphire, a variety of corundum which always exhibits a slight tinge of color and can thus be distinguished from synthetic colorless sapphire. Though leucosapphire is extremely rare, much rarer than even ruby and sapphire, yet it is much less valuable; for the beauty, and with it the value, of corundums lies in the splendor of their colors. These are caused by allochromatic coloration, that is to say, they owe their diverse hues to foreign pigmenting agents which occur as the finest metallic clouds distributed in the atomic lattice of the crystal. The saturation of hue is determined by the proportional content of these foreign coloring substances. Blue, brown, yellow, and green corundums are colored by iron, and in fact the oxidation valency of the iron is responsible for the distinct colors; in other words, trivalent

36

iron predominates in yellow and brown corundums, while divalent iron prevails in blue sapphires. In green sapphires divalent and trivalent iron probably occur in equal amounts. Each of these corundums has an iron content which, according to the intensity of its color, lies between 0.005 and 1 percent. The violet hues are caused by a vanadium content, which varies with the depth of color between 0.01 and 0.02 percent. As a curiosity the pinkish-orange colored *padparajah* (from *padmarajan* = lotus-blossom color) is superlative, enhanced by its unusual color and great rarity. The snowfields dyed by the last rays of the sinking sun offer a natural, very close match to its warm tones, which grade imperceptibly from soft orange to the most delicate salmon.

Besides these merits—a wealth of luxurious hues and vivid brilliance—corundums are also outstanding for one of the most bewildering light phenomena: asterism. By this is meant the image of a six-rayed star of light which appears to hover over the curved surface of a convex cabochon-cut stone and to glide over its surface when the stone is moved. The cause of this attractive phenomenon lies in the reflection of light by hair-fine rutile needles which, by so-called exsolution, have crystallized out in the interior of the corundum and arranged themselves parallel to the main crystallographic axes in three directions intersecting at 120 degrees. The arching of the surface above them concentrates the reflected light into three narrow lines, likewise crossing at 120 degrees in a central point. The phenomenon is particularly well displayed in the parallel beams of light from the sun or from an electric torch. The more densely the included rutile needles are ranged, the more marked appears the star. The sharpness of the star's rays determines the value of the stone. It is obvious that the transparency of star corundum is reduced by the presence of the rutile needles. The sharpest stars therefore appear on pale opaque corundums. Good stars on rubies and sapphires of saturated color are an extraordinary rarity, and such star stones are very costly.

Aluminium oxide, the crystalline basic substance of corundum, is fairly widely distributed in the earth's crust. Thus deposits of precious corundums are found in all continents, and the most important of them always include colored specimens. Famous for the variety of colors of their corundums are the fields at Ratnapura in Ceylon, as well as those near Mogok in Burma, near Chantaburi and Bo Ploi in Thailand, near Anakie in Queensland, Australia, in the Umba valley in Tanzania, and in Rock Creek and the Missouri River in the state of Montana. By far the most important occurrences of colored corundums are those in the widespread gemmiferous placers of Ceylon, from which gemstones have been recovered for thousands of years. These owe their origin to a new formation of minerals by contact metamorphism when, more than five hundred million years ago, pegmatite melts were forced up out of the white-hot fluid magma of the depths of the earth into cracks and fissures of the metamorphosed sedimentary mountains of Ceylon. Partly by contact alteration of country rock and the limestones interbedded with it, partly by the cooling of the hot melts, the most varied gemstones were formed. In this way the primary deposits originated in the interior of the mountains. Under the devastating effect of annually recurring monsoon rains, the mountains were weathered away, and the rock masses, eroded by the swollen rivers, were removed and carried away. Along with the rock debris, the gemstones too were transported away out of their comminuted mother rocks and laid down in the valley bottoms where, embedded in the river alluvials, they formed new secondary deposits.

Through this process, which lasted millions of years, a certain qualitative winnowing operated at the same time, in that the soft, and therefore worthless, rock was unable to resist this long and massive onslaught, and thus crumbled away. The hard minerals, on the other hand, collected in the gem-bearing beds, the so-called gem gravels (called *illam* by the natives), in rubble banks, in talus hills, in river beds, and everywhere where terraces formed on the hill slopes. The formation of these alluvial gem deposits was largely completed about a million years ago. They lie upon a much older, partly eroded bedrock, the former primeval surface of Ceylon.

The variety of these secondary occurrences leads to a like variety in methods of recovering the gemstones, namely river dredging on the one hand and surface or pit digging on the other. Both mining methods are, by our standards, extremely primitive. But all attempts at modernization have aroused the opposition of the inhabitants, who cling to the calling handed down to them over generations. The most valuable concentration of gemstones is found in the age-old river beds of the Kelani Ganga and Kalu Ganga, principally at the confluences of mountain streams, in embayments, and in the shallows of strong meanders. At such places the gem hunters erect a weir of brushwood transversely across the river, so that the water on the upstream side is dammed back and, within the faggot bundles, is forced into faster flow. Upstream of the weir a ditch is dug. In the fast-flowing water men with long-handled rakelike scrapers scoop the river detritus, draw it toward them, and heap it up in the ditch into a small dam, whence the flow of the water carries away the sand and other worthless sediment. In this way a first separation of the light material from the heavy valuable minerals is effected here. The buddler carries out a further winnowing. He loads the gem-bearing gravel collected up in the dam into a shallow basket, takes it to deep water, and rotates it with swaying movements in the water, so that the heavy minerals assemble on the bottom of the basket and the light ones are washed back into the river over its rim. The concentrate is thereafter examined by the sorters. This way of recovering gemstones from the rivers has remained unchanged in all its laboriousness in Ceylon for 2,500 years. Most of the gemstones found in Ceylon are cut there. The cutter—a picturesque figure—squats cross-legged at his cutting machine, which resembles a wooden bench standing upside-down, whose slotted props cradle a wooden spindle. On the left-hand end of this grooved wooden roller a thick lap of lead or tin is bolted, vertically. Shaft and cutting lap are moved back and forth by a slip-roped bow whose string runs around the shaft. One might think a musical instrument was being

22 With remarkable skill the Ceylonese transform unattractive pebbles into shining gemstones. They possess an extraordinarily good feeling for the correct cutting position, especially in cat's-eyes and star stones, but also in stones with irregularly distributed color.

played. With astonishing finger-tip sensitivity the cutter presses the rough gemstone against the cutting wheel, charging it now and then with an abrasive paste which he makes himself from carborundum and rice husks. From time to time he dips the stone in water, to cool and clean it, and examines the cut. Unfortunately in Ceylon the principle of always preserving as much of the weight of the rough stone as possible is still observed. For this reason most gems from Ceylon have to be recut in the West, to correct the clumsy form and to bring into full play the beauty of the precious stone by means of an ideal style of cut. Gemstones which are cut in cabochon form, for example, star stones and cat's-eyes, are cut and polished completely on this primitive contraption, on which finer cutting agents are gradually used. Transparent gemstones, on the other hand, which require a faceting lap, are only roughed out and then handed over roughly cut to the polisher. He sits at a lap bench whose horizontal copper lap is set in motion by a rope belt driven by a large wheel, the latter being hand-turned by an apprentice. He does not use just his fingers but an adjustable faceting device into which a so-called dop, holding the stone, can be bolted. In this manner he can give each facet the right angle and size. The cutting is not, as with diamond, governed by mathematical calculations, but rather by handed-down experience.

Ruby: Noblest of the Corundums

I_N extolling the proudest representative of the colored gemstones one is apt to reach a crescendo of enamored irrationality. Scarcely any other precious stone is able to arouse such emotional waves of enthusiasm as the ruby. To all peoples it has symbolized from time out of mind the highest of fortune's gifts—love. It endows children born in the month of July with priceless gifts, namely freedom, kindness, honor, and dignity. Ruby owes its personal popularity to the gorgeous glowing color of smoldering red fire beneath its shining, lacquerlike surface, and its name, derived from the Latin word *ruber* = red, denotes the embodiment of the most beautiful red. Light and velvety shades range from pink to darkest purple, but the crown of all beauty, the noblest and most precious nuance is pigeon blood red, a saturated shade of carmine red. The more glowing, the more vivid is the red sparkle, the choicer and more costly is the ruby.

But superlatives abound in the rational sphere, too. The "drop of Mother Earth's heart's blood," as ruby is dubbed in the imagery of the Orient, belongs together with sapphire to the royal family of the corundums. This means that it, too, consists of crystallized alumina (Al_2O_3) and thus possesses the same distinguishing properties: high hardness (9), high specific gravity (3.99), and high refractive index (1.765), which place it closely below diamond. Nevertheless, it has no need to acknowledge any master. The Indians clearly recognized this and named it, in Sanskrit, *ratnanavaka*, which means lord of the precious stones.

Ruby owes its fascinating color to an admixture of chromium oxide (Cr_2O_3: 0.02–0.6 percent, according to saturation), which immeasurably long ago nestled into the crystal lattice of the crystalline alumina and within it displaced a few parts per thousand of aluminium oxide. The color intensity is considerably influenced by the chromium content. The pigeon blood red mentioned above appears when 0.1 percent pure chromium oxide is present. If the oxidation valency of the chromium alters, when quadrivalent chromium partly replaces the normally trivalent one, the orange-tinted shades appear. Other nuances of red, such as brownish-red or violet, can be related to traces of iron and vanadium: a higher iron participation causes a brownish tinge, while the vanadium content imparts the blue tint. It is precisely this pigment, chromium—so rarely found in the upper regions of the earth's crust—which is responsible for the fact that ruby is one of the rarest precious stones. In other words, when ruby was formed, the very uncommon chance must have

23 Man's hand awakens the unimposing red
stones to the sparkling life of glowing rubies.

occurred that chromium oxide, originating from great depths in the earth, was present at exactly the right time when the alumina was crystallizing. Thus, in the knowledge of this rarity, ruby is the most costly of all the precious stones.

Ruby originates as a contact-metamorphic product of the pegmatitic-pneumatolytic phase. An almost classic example of this mode of origin is found in the mountainous surroundings of Mogok in Burma, where the most important ruby occurrences lie and whence the most beautiful rubies come. The mother rock is a white coarse-grained, partly dolomitic calcareous marble of very great age (over 500 million years), which is interbedded in crystalline schists. It is a contact rock which has resulted from the interaction of granitic magmas and alteration of limestone. It is known that the especially active pneumatolytic mineral solutions preferentially invade limestone and related calcareous country rocks and there give rise to the formation of new, surprisingly varied mineral suites. In this way the rich gemstone occurrences near Mogok have developed; and in the successive generations of gemstones crystallizing out one after another, ruby is the youngest, as it formed only when nothing but alumina and a little chromium oxide were left, out of all the dissolved substances. Chromium is normally not a constituent of rocks which participate in these segregation processes, but must have been brought up by melts which, rising from great depths at the right place and at the right time, became party to the crystallization of ruby. In the matrix rubies usually crop out in well-developed crystals. The blood-red specimens in white marble are a magnificent sight. For all that rubies occur very sparingly in primary deposits, they are in places very strongly concentrated in the weathered residue of the marble and the alluvial sediments formed from it in the valleys, whence they are mainly mined today.

The discovery of this very rich treasure trove of ruby round Mogok is lost in the obscurity of legend. It is said that a Burmese king in the fifteenth century obtained possession of the Mogok valley by cunning. A band of robbers, who were undergoing punishment for their crimes in the trackless valley, first reported the red stones. The king ordered the strictest secrecy. By the tortuous paths of diplomacy as already practiced then he obtained the rich Mogok valley from the unsuspecting Shan princes in exchange for a worthless piece of land, and was able to amass a fabulous treasure for the Burmese privy purse. A royal edict of the year 1597 contains the first known reference to the ruby fields of Mogok, which became the exclusive property of the Burmese throne. After Burma follow, as the discoveries ranking next, occurrences in Thailand, Cambodia, and Ceylon, in Tanzania, Afghanistan, and North Carolina. Even Switzerland contains a small ruby and sapphire deposit on the Campolungo in the Ticino River. Thailand is the second most important producer of rubies. The fields lie in the southeast, astride the frontier with Cambodia. They consist of extensive alluvial detritus of clayey gravels, which have been deposited from the erosion of contact metamorphosed limestones, and today lie many meters deep beneath beds of sandy loam. Siam rubies, which seldom attain the emphatic

24 In a few centuries the inhabitants of Mogok, where men and women, children and old folks are engaged in recovering, cutting and trading in rubies, have transformed the once green valley into a loamy brown field of diggings, and that not even with powerful excavating machines but with their own hands and the simple tools of their forefathers. To this day the lovely valleys between the green, jungle-covered hills throughout the whole district of Mogok swarm with colorfully dressed people digging for rubies; for the richest concentration of rubies is deep in the gem gravels of the detrital valley floors. From narrow shaftlike pits, or wide, deep mines, the treasures are hoisted to the surface for processing in the purposely built steplike washing places. Washed from the collecting basin into the progressively lower settling bins, the heavy minerals settle at the bottom of the latter.

color impact of Burma rubies, are darker and often violet or brown tinted. Lovelier, again, are the rubies from Pailin (Cambodia). The mainly light to raspberry red Ceylon rubies, which are characterized by a specially brilliant luster, are mined in the southwest of the island near Ratnapura, from gem gravels, in the manner described under corundum and chrysoberyl. Specimens are usually so light that it is difficult to distinguish between light red rubies and deeply colored pink sapphires. Recently the ruby occurrences in Tanzania have enjoyed increased notice. In the valley of the Umba River, which runs into the Indian Ocean between Tanga in Tanzania and Mombasa in Kenya, beautiful clear rubies, whose color may be likened to that of Siam rubies, await recovery from primary and secondary deposits, along with multicolored corundums. Further northwest, at the foot of the Matabatu Hills, native miners excavate from two small mines large, nontransparent but deep red rubies embedded in green zoisite rock. These small but strongly colored rubies are in the main excellent for use in jewelry.

Although the distinguishable color nuances for the various occurrences are ostensibly typical, the colors are never valid as evidence of origin. The many source names used in the trade as indications of quality, such as Burma ruby, Siam ruby, and so forth, are misleading and undependable, because each deposit produces both top quality and mediocre rubies. One of the keys to the origin and real understanding of ruby, however, which may provide reliable evidence, is its inclusions. These are hardly ever absent; for flawless rubies are extremely seldom found. Almost always they contain foreign microcrystals. These have either originated from the surrounding matrix, or have grown along with the ruby, or have subsequently crystallized out as so-called rutile needles. The rutile needles form an extremely fine network, called "silk," which gives rise to a delicate silvery shimmer of light which, on rubies cut with a convex shape, may coalesce into a star. Other inclusions are streamers of fluid droplets, which in their delicate, weblike arrangement resemble dragon-fly wings. Inclusions serve as undeniable proofs of origin, by means of which the genuine, earthborn ruby may be distinguished from the synthetic (man-made) product. Our technology enables us to fabricate stones of such identical chemical, physical, and optical properties that only the type of inclusions provides sure proof of their origin. In contrast to diamond, in which highest quality can be conferred by greatest clarity, the inclusions of ruby, as with other colored gemstones, offer valuable evidence of genuineness.

Likewise in contrast with diamonds, not many rubies have made history, for here Nature was not nearly so bountiful as in the case of diamonds; rubies occur extremely seldom as large crystals. Specimens of more than 5 carats are very rare, and those of 10 or more carats are exceptions to the rule. Many such stones are in the possession of oriental princes, for Eastern superstition credits rubies with magic qualities; amongst others, they are said to give man the power to predict terrible calamities. When evil is encountered, rubies are said to darken, but lighten again after the time of misfortune has passed.

In regard to their usual small size, it sounds like a fairy tale to hear of a ruby of 138 carats weight. And yet this crystal wonder appeared in visible form in the Rosser Reeves ruby, which was donated a few years ago to the Smithsonian Institution in Washington, D.C. It is a star ruby of perfect shape, and as large as a walnut. The Delong ruby, of 100 carats, in the Natural History Museum in New York was not long ago the victim of a robbery until, in return for a high ransom, it was recovered again from a telephone booth. In the Armistice year of 1918 the last large ruby was found. It received the name Peace ruby, and weighed 41 carats; it is an exceptionally beautiful specimen.

25 The concentrate is scooped out by hand, for spreading out on the sorting table. Squatting at the sorting table, the sorter, with scarcely contained excitement, takes out from a multitude of worthless pebbles a few tiny red sparkling grains and puts them carefully away in a silk purse. As reward for his tedious work the earth has given him a few small rubies. On the primitive cutting benches, whose laps are foot-driven, the rubies receive their richly faceted cut form.

Sapphire: Lord Keeper of the Seals in the Gem Kingdom

*I*N the close mesh of fiction and truth sapphire is more closely ensnared than any of its noble peers. Out of mankind's long acquaintance with it, towers of Babylonian dimensions have pressed heavily on its brazen back, built out of the tough ashlar of pagan and Christian magic, which sought to make use of supernatural powers through the stone of heavenly blue. In fact, sapphire was for centuries the chosen jewel of princes of the church and worldly rulers, whose treasure hoards still show testimony of this.

Many languages acted as godparents at its baptism. In Sanskrit sapphire was called *sauriratna,* meaning "sacred to Saturn." In Chaldean it was called *sampir,* in Greek *sappheiros,* in Latin *saphirus,* and in Arabic *safir*—names which corroborate its wide distribution. It is indisputable that the blue sapphire is far more plentiful than its nobler brother, the red ruby, and in places so much so that, as with diamond, inferior qualities find use as abrasives.

Close family ties bind sapphire to ruby, and just as ancient as the veneration of the one, is the esteem in which the other is held. Yet, while the high-spirited, fiery brother courts the favor of dark women in such princely fashion, the quieter, more modest sapphire enjoys the affection of all women, especially of blondes. As an aristocratic descendant of the same family, sapphire commands the same properties as ruby, for sapphire too is a corundum and is composed of aluminium oxide (Al_2O_3). It shares with the other corundums the same values for refractive index, specific gravity, and hardness. Created out of identical matter, the occurrence of blue sapphire is frequently associated with that of ruby. Burma's soil sometimes yields a capricious combination of both, namely, sapphire with plum blue center inside a red mantle.

If ruby may lay claim to the finest color in the world in its most outstanding manifestation, so sapphire, while contenting itself with the more restrained blue, nevertheless compensates for this unpretentiousness with a much more sumptuous wealth of shades. The lovely cornflower blue is the most coveted hue, soft and velvety, scintillating yet bland at the same time; it is a clear, deep blue, enhanced by a gentle admixture of kingly purple. Scarcely less outstanding is the royal blue sapphire. A delicate coat of silken velvet sheen spreads over it, leading the glance into its hidden depths, rendered as unfathomable as mountain lakes by a tiny trace of cobalt blue. Of enchanting

46

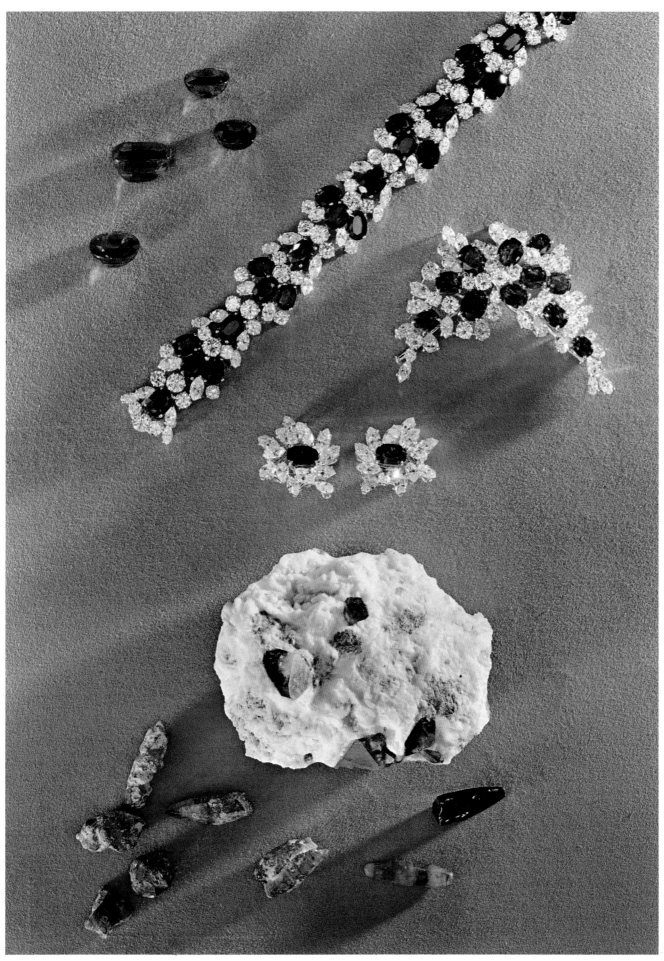

26 No gemstone symbolizes the color
of fidelity better than blue sapphire.

27 Women gem washers discuss their day's production in the Mogok valley, Burma.

beauty and nearly as valuable is the marine blue sapphire, dazzling yet warmly radiant crystallized drops of the deep blue oriental ocean. But that is not all: the shades span from dense, dark gentian blue to crystal-clear ice blue, from dancing, frivolous azure blue, through pale, cheerful sky blue, to crackling, exciting electric blue. One's vocabulary seems too paltry to do justice to the many possible variants of blue. Nature has been so inventive in them that it seems presumptuous to speak of sapphire blue as a conception of one quite definite color. Likewise it is unsuitable to express the variety of shades provided by Nature in terms of source; for she scatters light and dark, pure and particolored sapphire in all corundum deposits, without exception. It might also be worth asking why one should grant one's preference only to the cornflower hue solely because it, being the rarest, commands the highest monetary value. Do not all sapphires harbor in themselves the reflected blues of the heavens at all times of day and throughout all parts of the earth?

The wonderful blue of the falling shades of coming nightfall, never attained by any other natural stone, is imparted to sapphire by submicroscopic traces of foreign substances: iron and titanium oxides. The main pigment responsible for the blue color is divalent iron.

48

While its discernible content of 0.01 to 1 percent determines the strength of color, the subordinate titanium influences the fine nuances and is thus clearly the cause of the differences which determine value, between cornflower, royal, marine blue, and so on. The reason for the greater frequency of blue sapphire than of ruby also lies in the coloring matter, that is to say, in the far wider distribution of titanium-iron compounds in the upper rock-forming regions of the earth's crust, in which the birthplace of sapphire lies. Like rubies, most sapphires may be considered contact minerals. As such, they have developed as accessory minerals of an extensive contact metamorphism, when granitic magmas rose

28 In the very prolific sapphire deposits near Kanburi and Bang-Kha-Cha in Thailand and Pailin in Cambodia, which were discovered between the midnineteenth and twentieth centuries by migrant Burmese, the extraction methods introduced by them have scarcely changed. Often the fields of diggings lie in abandoned banana or rubber plantations. The deep, narrow excavations are usually small family concerns. In many places they are connected up together by crawling tunnels. At depth a man digs up the riches of the earth and heaps the spoil into plaited bamboo baskets. At the top a woman looks after the bamboo hoists, to which the baskets are attached when full.

into preexisting old limestones, converting them into coarse-grained marbles and at the same time delivering the ingredients for the formation of new minerals. Often, however, sapphire appears to have been more closely connected with a purely pegmatitic formation process, as indicated by several characteristic pegmatite minerals found inside it. As with ruby, so with sapphire the inclusions are determined by the mode of its origin and structure. Its interior life is a wonder world in the tiniest space; its reputation that of an hospitable host who accommodates his guests forever. In favorable circumstances it encloses individual gemstones of microscopic size, which crystallized before or simultaneously with it. It is one of Nature's whimsical tricks that titanium oxide (TiO_2), which is incorporated in colloidal state as a coloring agent, also exists in crystalline form as finest rutile needles, producing the so-called silk, from which many gleaming iridescent reflections twinkle. This playful caprice of winking Nature culminates in enchanting magic when the silvery glint of asterism shimmers over the silken blue background.

The most important sapphire occurrences are found in Ceylon, Burma, Thailand, Tanzania, Cambodia, Australia, and in the state of Montana. Recovery is principally from alluvial detrital debris, though in places directly from the matrix, too. Near Kyaukpyatthat in Burma, in the Umba valley in Tanzania, and near Yogo Gulch in Montana, both primary and secondary deposits are mined at the same time and adjacent to one another. In each case, however, the placers prove far the more productive. In Burma and Ceylon excavation is carried out in the manner described under corundum, ruby, chrysoberyl and spinel. In Indochina the sapphire deposits are in coarse-grained alluvial gravel banks, which have developed from weathered basalts. They are exceptionally rich in black star sapphires, in addition to which blue, yellow, green, and pink sapphires, garnets, zircons, and black spinels are obtained. The most beautiful sapphires, however, come from Pailin, though they are generally smaller than those of Burma or Ceylon.

Rome and Egypt prized the sapphire as the sacred stone of truth and justice; to the Buddhists it signifies peace, friendship, and steadfastness, and is therefore worn as a talisman for conjugal happiness. The sapphire was admitted very early by the Christian church. Innocent III decreed in a papal bull that every cardinal and bishop should wear a sapphire ring on his right, i.e., blessing hand. Strangely enough, at the same time the sapphire was the medium of the necromancers who believed that through it they would receive power to hear voices and to foretell the future. Moreover, from time immemorial mankind has considered it the stone of chastity and fidelity.

Crown jewels of all lands vied for the privilege of being able to scintillate with "tears from the eyes of the Goddess Saitya." She must have been a sad goddess to whom the Hindus prayed, for she wept many and large tears. But the teardrops of the gods were not used only in majestic regalia, as in the eighteenfold decoration of the famous crown of the Bohemian King Wenceslas. In the United States another idea originated. From three magnificent sapphires, each of which weighed about 2,000 carats, the heads of Presidents

Abraham Lincoln, George Washington, and General Eisenhower were carved. But paying homage to our forebears is today occasionally contrasted with profane desecration. Around the Stuart sapphire—a heart-shaped stone surrounded by sixteen diamonds—which the unhappy Queen of Scots gave to her consort, Lord Darnley, is entwined a bloody history. In the mineralogical gallery of the Natural History Museum in Paris the 136-carat violet sapphire of Louis XIV ekes out an unnoticed existence—*sic transit gloria mundi* ("thus passes away the glory of this world"). In New York the Star of India, a majestic star sapphire of 535 carats with a diameter of 4 cm., glitters in the Natural History Museum. The Russian State Treasury shelters a 260-carat Ceylon sapphire of light blue, the color preferred above all others by the last czarina. The largest star sapphire known till now, 63,000 carats, was found in Burma in October 1966.

As birthstone, sapphire is allotted to September. The qualities: peace of mind, sagacity, and fidelity are the felicitous gifts bestowed by its possession.

29 The gem-bearing gravels are dumped near the mouth of the pit. From time to time the miner squats down on them and searches through the mine spoil with a scythelike tool. Only where water is available are they washed. A lovely variety of corundum occurring here is the yellow- and blue-, as well as green- and yellow-banded sapphire. As elsewhere, there are varying qualities here, too.

Beryl: Palette of Pastel Colors

BEHIND this chromatic-sounding description shelters another gemstone family of astonishingly manifold colors, even though few people are aware of them. The name is probably of Indian origin, for it is derived from the Prakrit word *veruliyam* and has come down to us via the Latin *berullus*. In olden times, so Pliny reports in his *Historia Naturalis*, beryls were used as eyeglasses. The Emperor Nero is reputed to have watched gladiatorial fights through an emerald, the rarest and most precious member of the beryl group. In the Middle Ages beryl also served as a magic mirror in which one might foresee the future. Monstrances and reliquary caskets were made at that time with cut slices of beryl, which displayed the holy relics in peculiar radiance. Strife, brawling, and injury did not occur when beryl was worn; as a symbol of purity it was supposed to protect the innocent. Liquids in which it had lain were considered not only nonpoisonous but as effective healing potions against weakness and pains of the internal organs.

Beryls are characteristic minerals of the pegmatites, those thin fluid melts which, in rising into the seams and fissures of older rocks, carried with them all the substances necessary to the formation of beryls. The latter belong to the large group of silicates. Silica (Si_6O_{18}) forms so-called six-rings, which are firmly bonded together by means of the beryllium and aluminium oxide molecules (3 BeO and 1 Al_2O_3) situated between them. This leads to a combination between beryllia and alumina with silica $[Be_3Al_2(SiO_3)_6]$. This close bonding between the architectural building blocks of the crystal results in good resistance to mechanical wear (hardness $= 7.5 - 8$). All other properties such as specific gravity (2.72) and refractive index (1.58) are fairly low. For its feeble brilliance, despite its lively vitreous luster, beryl finds a worthy compensation in the individuality of its pastel colors.

Beryls, like most gemstones, provide a typical example of allochromatic coloring, for when they are of the pure chemical composition explained above they are colorless. It is characteristic of a pegmatitic mineral that it takes up, from all the countless volatile components of the parent melt, all those which may contribute to the enhancement of its beauty. Beryl is no exception. An absolute mine of such rare elements, which have improved all its properties, is the rose red beryl. There is no stone to be compared with it for loveliness when, besides the delicate peach-blossom tint, it sometimes attains a fine cyclamen red. The sometimes amazingly intense pink originates from the rare metal cesium, reinforced by manganese. The gemmologist G. F. Kunz, of the New York firm of

30 From large, clear beryl crystals
magnificent gemstones can be cut.

31 In the quarrylike open-cast mine of a primary deposit of aquamarine near Pedra Azul in Minas Gerais, Brazil, miners are in the process of breaking up the matrix (pegmatite).

Tiffany, christened it morganite in honor of the American gemstone Maecenas, J. P. Morgan. The youthful blue of aquamarine is due to a trace of divalent iron.

These water-clear jewels from the nymphs' treasure chests were strewn—so runs the myth—by sea horses on the shores where man dwelt. Lake green or sea blue, of the transparent clarity of all beryls, aquamarine is always linked in its legends with water: It accompanies seafarers and ensures them a landfall free from danger; and around the little ship of marital happiness it twines the bond of fidelity. Aquamarine is the stone of all young people, and takes the March-born under its protection. It is trivalent iron which pours the color of liquid gold into the warmly sparkling golden beryl, while a mixture of divalent and trivalent iron induces green shades. The sun-yellow heliodor could hardly have been more aptly named by the natives of South Africa than "gift of the sun." In all seriousness they assert that this rare gemstone fell to earth with a mighty rain of meteorites. The color is based on a tiny admixture of uranium oxide, which makes it so irresistible to collectors.

As the favorite children of pegmatites, those zealous producers of gemstones, beryls are accessory to many gem deposits in all continents, principally in Ceylon and Madagascar, in Burma, India, and California, as well as in the Urals. But much the most important finds of beryl lie in Brazil in the gem-rich states of Bahia, Espirito Santo, and Minas Gerais. Here they are found in coarse-grained pegmatites and their weathered relicts; also in crystalline schists, mostly together with other characteristic minerals of pegmatitic paragenesis such as topaz, tourmaline, and many others; in druses; and finally in quartz lodes which traverse granites, gneisses, and mica schists. From these primary deposits beryls are recovered by the working of individual quarries and, in many places also, by open cast mining. As beryls are derived from thin fluid melts, huge crystals have often been able to develop, attaining up to 2 meters in length and 3 tons in weight. The gem gravels arising from the existing country rocks, in slope scree and as boulders, are loosened up wherever these detrital mounds have consolidated, by powerful jets of water until they crumble. The pebbles loosened in this way are thereafter, like the loose detritus, collected up with shovels and rakes and washed in streams flowing nearby. From the interior of the country they go, for cutting, to Rio de Janeiro or Idar-Oberstein (Germany), the two most important trading centers for Brazilian gemstones.

Prices for beryls vary very widely according to color and quality. The light specimens are much cheaper than the deeply colored; similarly the clear stones are dearer than the cloudy ones.

32 Near Teofilo Otoni in the state of Minas Gerais, Brazil, gemstone hunters loosen the detrital masses of eluvial sediments of an aquamarine-bearing gem gravel by means of a strong jet of water.

Emerald: Symbol of Verdant Spring

"WE find enjoyment, it is true, in the agreeable green of grass and leaves, but incomparably greater is the pleasure of beholding an emerald; for its green is the most satisfying of all," so Pliny extolled the aristocratic chieftain of the beryl family. Nevertheless, the reader has the feeling that even Pliny, despite his telling description, was at a loss to give an adequate picture of the emerald's beauty. It will not surprise anyone to know that here, too, chromium oxide is once again the decisive ingredient that imparts this matchless green to emeralds. In fact, only those beryls in which chromium is the coloring agent rank as emeralds. Yet minimal traces of chromium suffice to produce the unique emerald color, which distinguishes it sharply from the beryls colored green by iron. The intensity of color depends on the magnitude of the chromium content. On the other hand, the trace elements which frequently accompany chromium—iron and vanadium—give rise to the yellow and bluish tones. The delicate shades of an extremely subtle palette grade from pale leaf green through melancholy fir green. The best and most precious color is the dewy green of fresh spring grass, intense and clear, which even the gay blandishments of electric light on festive occasions cannot budge from its natural coloring.

In the atomic lattice of beryllium aluminium silicate, which represents the chemical composition of beryl, each trivalent chromium oxide atom replaces one of aluminium oxide. As its volume is greater than that of alumina, the bond between the silicate rings is weakened and the brittleness appropriate to each mineral is increased. Thus emerald, despite its hardness of 7.5–8, is more sensitive to mechanical shock than other gemstones of equal hardness. It needs therefore to be handled and worn with special care. Moreover, the easily induced inner tensions favor the formation of inclusions, and consequently flawless emeralds of more than one carat seem to belong to legend. But no one would care to dispense with the attractive enclosures which light up the stone from the inside like tiny bright suns. The charming inclusions and obscurities are of varied nature. They are mostly fine channels, which contain minute quantities of fluids, or jagged cavities in whose liquids float a gas bubble and a tiny salt crystal—permanent witnesses housed in their precious dwelling from the time of its birth. Again, they are often microscopic crystallites, taken over from the matrix or grown with the host crystal in the most intimate contact—visible to the eye as mosslike designs. Likening them to peaceful, sun-dappled garden foliage, the poetic description *jardin* (garden) has been adopted. Is it not bordering on presumption to speak of flaws in the presence of such marvels of nature? Anyone seeking to find faults in

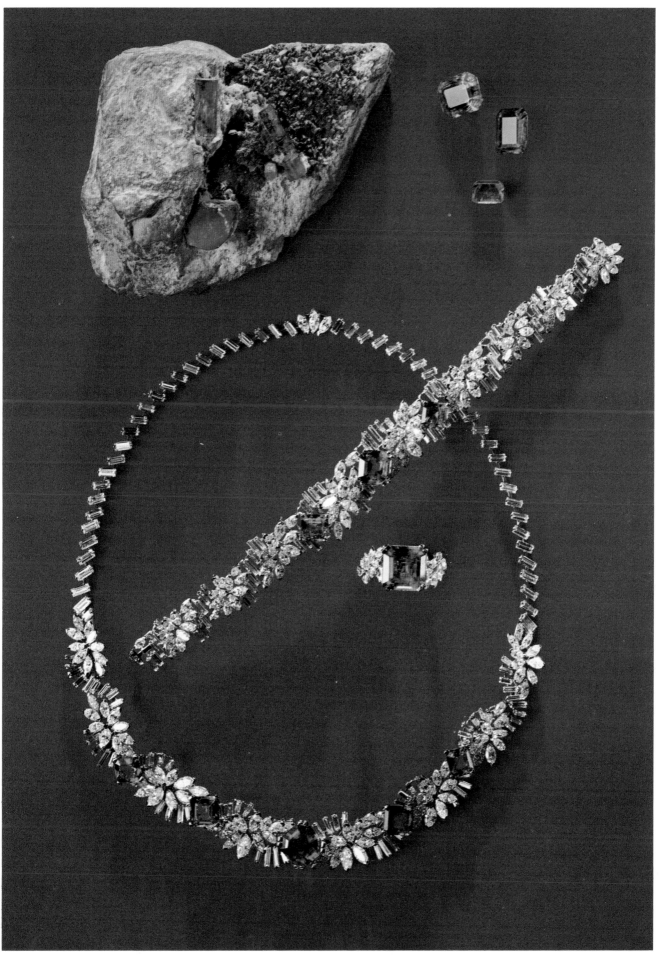

33 From the raw environment of the earth's womb to its majestic sparkle
in a brilliant jewel, the emerald undergoes a glorious transformation.

the manifold diversity of inanimate Nature's forms mistakes her true being; for she tolerates no incompleteness, and everything she brings forth has its own appointed purpose.

With its siblings of the beryl family emerald shares the same low physical properties. The tranquil calm of its green is enhanced by its low refractive index, and, as it is almost always dug from its matrix and not from gem gravels, it has no need of a high specific gravity either.

It is no wonder that tales and legends have always been closely and often inseparably interwoven with this treasure of the earth. We know that Caesar collected emeralds because of their fabled healing power, and still today this stone can be found in pseudomedical literature as the so-called healing stone. A 225-carat emerald, in American possession, bears the portrait of this great Roman commander in chief. Charlemagne's crown and the famous iron crown of the Lombards were set with emeralds. At his enthronement in the year 1171 Henry II, King of the Irish, received an exceptional emerald ring, as symbol of his power. Right into the late Middle Ages emeralds were of the most extreme rarity and of boundlessly high value; for they all originated from the only two deposits known then, in Jebel Sikait (Egypt) and in the Habach Valley (Austria). But this changed noticeably when the Spanish conquistadores Cortez and Pizarro landed in South America in the sixteenth century and an untold wealth of emeralds, stolen from the palaces and temples of the Aztecs and Incas, flowed into the Old World. A contemporary chronicler reports an emerald of the size of a hen's egg, which was held in godlike honor. From one unique huge crystal is cut the pride of the Viennese treasure: an emerald jar 4 inches high and weighing 2,680 carats, which was acquired by the Hapsburgs in the seventeenth century. At an auction in Bern a few years ago the captivating emerald parure of the Empress Eugénie came up for sale. Napoleon III's lover's knot surrounds nine large emeralds of between 14 and 23 carats each. The greatest collection of emeralds, however, embellishes the crown of The Holy Virgin Mary, Queen of the Andes, which was publicly shown in Europe for the first time in September 1968. The crown was endowed in 1593 by the people of the Colombian town of Popayán as a thank-offering for their preservation from a three-year pestilence. Twenty-four gold-smiths worked continuously for six years to make the finely chiselled and richly ornamented Crown of the Andes from one massive gold nugget. This splendid jewel is adorned with 453 emeralds of a total weight of 1,521 carats. Today, each carat attains a valuation price of $3,000. After a long odyssey this treasure, estimated to be the most valuable in the world, landed in the United States a few years ago. These gems scarcely ever came directly from their source; for neither torture nor fear of death was able to prize from the Inca priests the secret of their emerald localities. On the contrary, in their boundless thirst for revenge, they obliterated every trace. The work of destruction was carried out so completely that in the end it was by chance that the Muzo mine—the most

34 Miners break up the loose rocks of an emerald deposit with crowbars.

productive hoard of today's most splendid emeralds—was rediscovered, and only at the beginning of the present century was the Chivor mine near the village of Somondoco found. The other emerald deposits known today in Colombia have been gradually made accessible.

The allure and aura of this mysterious green precious stone are further magnified when one realizes that in millions of years a chance concatenation of circumstances must have occurred in the earth's interior in order to have given birth to this gem. The overwhelming majority of emerald occurrences belong to the pegmatitic phase, although in fact the most important deposit at Muzo can hardly be credited to it entirely; it seems rather to fall in a transition stage between the pegmatitic and hydrothermal phases. The growth cavities of the emeralds are here located in unmetamorphosed sedimentary calcareous shales, whose age of 130 million years reaches back to the Lower Cretaceous Period. Pegmatites are present deep underground and indicate the proximity of the magma. The emerald-bearing veins which traverse the calcareous shales seem to have been

35 At the Somerset emerald mine in the Transvaal the emeralds are
loosened from their matrix in huge concentration plants, and, underneath,
are picked by hand from the conveyor belt by sharp-eyed workers.

formed near the surface and therefore under relatively low pressure; they contain many
druses of varying sizes. The emerald crystals have grown inside them from hydrothermal
solutions, often very freely, and thus are well developed. Many individual ones are
relatively clear. The accessory minerals, apatite, fluorite, and barite, which are profusely
present, indicate a hydrothermal content in the solutions.

The emeralds of Chivor, the other major occurrence in Colombia, originate in a
hard, metamorphic matrix, which in its composition approaches a pegmatite. It crops out
in veins and gangues which often widen out into considerable cavities. The emeralds
which have grown in them, mostly unhindered, show well-formed crystals. Unfortunately
they are somewhat paler than the deeply colored Muzo crystals because of a lower
chromium content. Little is known of the geological conditions of the other Colombian
emerald occurrences—Burbar, Cosquez, Gachala, and so on. It appears, however, that
they resemble those of Chivor rather than those of Muzo.

All other emerald deposits of the world differ from these rather atypical Colombian occurrences in their connection with chrome-bearing metamorphic schists. The emerald deposits of the Urals—for ninety years the most important after the Colombian ones but today without importance—are situated on the Siberian side of the mountain chain on the Tokowaya River northeast of Sverdlovsk, the former Ekaterinburg, where in the night of 16th/17th July 1918 the Czar and his family were murdered. There, in 1831 after a storm-lashed night, a considerable number of emeralds were found in the roots of a fallen tree. The matrix is a biotite mica schist, which is penetrated by talc and chlorite schists and which has been contact metamorphosed by a nearby granite massif and intrusive pegmatites. The accessory minerals are typical of the pegmatitic-pneumatolytic phase. Those minerals, however, which in Colombia suggest a transition to the hydrothermal phase, are completely lacking. The many large emerald crystals are mostly of poor color and dull. Only the small specimens have good colors.

Conditions are similar in the emerald deposits in South Africa, Rhodesia, and in the Habachtal in the Austrian Alps where pegmatites have intruded extensively into mica schists. The pegmatites brought beryllia and alumina as well as silica, while the chromium originated in the mostly greenish mica schists. Significantly the deep green specimens are found predominantly in the mica schists. The emeralds of South Africa and from the Habachtal are very similar to those of the Urals, while the Sandawana emeralds from Rhodesia excel in their fresh, lively green, which very soon after their discovery in the year 1956 brought them into favor with the connoisseur.

Emerald is one of the few gemstones which is mined from its matrix, in other words, from primary deposits. At most emerald mines the exploitation methods are still extremely primitive. The unusual mode of occurrence does not allow a simple cleaning out of the irregularly spaced gangues and cavities, but rather the whole solid rock must be mined so as not to risk overlooking possible rich pockets by a few centimeters. Nearly all mines are therefore exploited by open cast methods. Over a whole mountainside or round a whole hill steps or terraces are cut. The miners stand in a row with their backs to the hill slope and plunge 3-meter long crowbars, weighing 15 kg., into the relatively crumbly rock. The front end of the bar is pointed to enable better penetration into the ground, and the other is wedge shaped and tapering, to break up the rock. In the Cobra/Somerset occurrence near Gravelotte in the Transvaal (South Africa) massive pegmatite cones have pushed up into mica schists and have led to emerald formation. Here the most modern mining methods and installations are used.

Chrysoberyl: The Three Dissimilar Brothers

SELDOM properly valued by laymen, but an inexhaustible source of wonderful delight to collectors, are the chrysoberyls. Little known, jealously hoarded by the earth and only yielded up in parsimonious numbers, they are assured of a prominent place among the gemstones. Their great rarity, combined with their three varieties, completely different from one another, has rendered them prized objects of desire. Alexandrite and cat's-eye, two varieties as precious as they are strangely attractive, are the basis of the chrysoberyls' fame.

The simple, transparent chrysoberyl, whose name, derived from the Greek *chrysos* = gold, indicates that it contains beryllium, but actually consists of equal parts of beryllia (BeO) and alumina (that is, corundum, Al_2O_3) and is thus a beryllium aluminate ($BeAl_2O_4$). This combination crystallizes in well-formed prisms, which evince an irresistible tendency to grow in that form as trillings, which result in a star-shaped figure or crystal with six-sided circumference (see color plate opposite, top right). Gay, and even a little frivolous, they sparkle in shades of finch yellow to lime green via deep chartreuse and olive green to warm, smoky, golden tobacco tones. In all these alluring colors we have once again an allochromatic or extraneous coloring agent, for the combination of the two molecules of beryllium and aluminium oxides is by itself colorless. As color-producing metals, iron (up to 6 percent Fe_2O_3) and chromium (only 0.6 percent Cr_2O_3) have been proved. Titanium is found occasionally in mere traces. Thanks to great hardness (8.5) chrysoberyl takes a good polish, resulting in a strong surface luster which, jointly with high refractive index (1.75), produces a very lively brilliance. The likewise high specific gravity (3.71) favors its concentration in river debris, i.e., in secondary deposits. All these properties place chrysoberyl immediately next to corundum, with whose similarly colored specimens it can easily be confused.

The chatoyant variety of chrysoberyl—the silken-sheened cat's-eye—is of an unusual nature, for it is characterized by a very striking and at the same time singularly beautiful play of light, which, allied with the rarity of its occurrence, is the reason for its popularity with collectors. Over the surface hovers a silvery band of light, whose apparent detachment from the body of the stone seems mysterious and magical. At the slightest

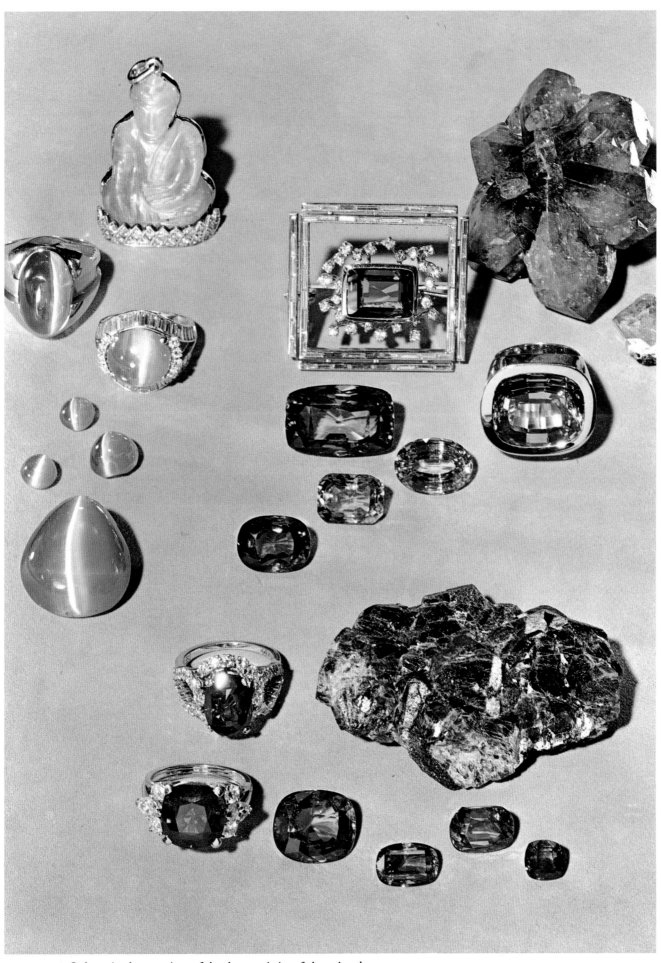

36 Only a visual comparison of the three varieties of chrysoberyl can
clarify their baffling differences. Cat's-eye, chrysoberyl, and alexandrite.

turn of the stone the line of light leaps into surging movement; leaving its static position, flitting swiftly like a lissom cat, it glides—as if divorced from reality—over the domed surface. This wondrous phenomenon is caused by reflection of the incident light from hair-fine parallel fibers in the interior of the stone. The ribbon of reflected light always runs at right angles to the alignment direction of the embedded fibers. Cat's-eyes are normally cut *en cabochon* because the bright band of light is best evoked in this way. By means of the convex external shape it is narrowed to a sharp track of light, comparable to the slit-shaped pupils of cats' eyes. The narrower and more precise the trace of the line of light, the greater the value. Occasionally other kinds of gemstones show a similar chatoyancy. But of all these varieties, likewise named cat's-eyes, chrysoberyl is not only the noblest but also the most valuable. Its personal name *cymophane* (derived from the Greek *kyma* = wave, and *phanein* = to appear) differentiates it from its less distinguished cousins. It is strange that the cymophane, despite its ghostly appearance, has never given rise to any myths, for surprisingly no superstitious emotion has been attached to it.

A gemstone so truly unusual and mysterious as alexandrite—the third of the chrysoberyl brothers—which, though unpretentious, appeals to the predilection of connoisseurs, well deserves a place in the limelight. Here it may display, with most marvellous magic, its salient property of changing its color chameleonlike between daylight and artificial light. In fact, alexandrite is not only one of the most costly gemstones in the world, but also one of the most remarkable; for daylight discloses its gentle moss green, with a vaguely bluish suffusion, which changes to raspberry red or amethyst purple in or under artificial lighting. Its color is a characteristic chromium pigmentation; however, the cause of the phenomenal day-and-night magic does not lie in the chromium's changing by different light, but results from the composition of the light. Daylight contains mainly blue rays, artificial light is rich in red. The color predominating at the time is reflected from the alexandrite. Thus it constitutes an extreme example of the so-called day-and-night stones, whose color appears different according to the lighting. It is consequently appreciated by connoisseurs who know its secret. It was discovered in the thirties of the last century on the slopes of the Urals northeast of Ekaterinburg, ostensibly on the occasion of the coming of age of the later Czar Alexander II, and was named alexandrite in honor of him. At first alexandrite was considered to be the Russian national stone, since it combined the Czarist colors. Apart from its striking color change and its extreme rarity because of its chromium content, alexandrite also furnishes, from a genetic viewpoint, an interesting case of fortuitousness. It is, in spite of its chromium coloring, a mineral of pegmatitic-pneumatolytic origin and was formed when beryllium-rich solutions, dispersing from pegmatites, penetrated the surrounding mica schists, initiating the formation of three different beryllium minerals at the edge of the pegmatites. These are the beryllium silicate phenakite, the beryllium-aluminium silicate emerald, and finally the beryllium aluminate chrysoberyl. Interestingly, the minerals within the pegmatite are

37 Bamboo scaffolding reveals the presence of a gemstone pit in Ceylon.

colorless, while those in the mica schists are green. It therefore follows that the chromium, originally present in the mica schists, has moved into the contact zone and here led to the formation of alexandrite (and, naturally, emerald also). The phenakite originating in the pegmatite is entirely free from pigmenting agents and is therefore colorless. For almost a hundred years the Urals produced by far the most beautiful alexandrites with a velvety bluish-green daylight color, and a very intense color change. Today the deposit is completely neglected. The latest discovery in Rhodesia, which produces a very similar quality, adjoins near Novello in the northeast the richly chrome-bearing mica schist zone of the Novello, Sandawana, and Filabusi emerald deposits.

Other important sources are the gem gravels in Brazil and Ceylon, of which the latter are the more interesting, since they yield all three varieties of chrysoberyl in all their respective colors. The matrix is a granitic pegmatite in the central massif of the island, from which they have been removed by erosion and deposited in secondary occurrences of the age-old river sediments. Here they are dug out of the river beds in the same manner as

38 The working of gem-bearing *illam* beds is not finished with just one layer, for barren detritus always lies in between. Consequently the miner often excavates several illam layers, of which the last and geologically oldest is usually the richest. He piles the loose gem gravel into baskets, which are hauled up out of the shaft with a windlass and, after being separated from the unproductive spoil, it is emptied on to an ever-growing pile of illam. This very strenuous work may last weeks or even months, and meanwhile the precious soil of the illam pile must be continuously guarded.

that described under corundum. Much richer are the alluvial valley bottoms which were laid down over millions of years. One can recognize the discovery places from afar, where bamboo scaffolds or small huts rise from rice paddies. At all these locations a gem hunter will have started digging, with his helpers, on a day said to be favorable by the soothsayer, and after a previous sacrifice to the supernatural powers. The excavated shafts attain a depth of up to 15 meters in the sandy-loamy soil before the gem-bearing *illam* concentrations are reached. These illam beds lie in irregular layers from a few centimeters to 1.5 meters thick, one above the other, and their horizontal width may reach 10 centimeters to two meters and extend up to a hundred meters in length. The illam is easily recognized because it is always accompanied by fine-grained to coarse quartz gravels. At the bottom of the pit a miner scrapes away the soil and gradually widens the excavation until all the intersected illam strata have been used up. Before starting work on the first washing day—once again determined by the astrologer—the owner distributes, instead of the earlier sacrifice to the gods, symbolic alms to his treasure seekers. The overseer

39 The puddlers fill their conically woven baskets at the pile of illam and carry them to the wash pool. Here they stand up to their waists in the muddy water and rotate their baskets so skillfully that all light and worthless material is floated over the edge of the basket, while the heavy gemstones—chrysoberyl, garnet, corundum, spinel, topaz, tourmaline, zircon, and many others—collect in the deepest part of the basket as so-called "dullam." The washer fills and washes his basket several times until sufficient dullam has collected in it. Then he places the basket in front of the overseer and the exciting moment has come.

crouches by the accumulated baskets, says a short and fervent prayer to Kataragama, the god of minerals, and then with skillful hand movements and sharp practiced eyes searches through the remaining concentrate. With sure expert glance, it is amazing how he recognizes the valuable stones from among the unattractive colored pebbles. Finally, with attentive demeanor and critical look, he lets the separated rough stones run once more through his fingers before he hands over the basket of remaining less valuable *dullam* to the washer for his own disposal. It is always fascinating to watch all these work stages from excavation, via recovery, to cutting on the swiftly spinning cutting lap, and to observe how an earthborn rough pebble is turned by man's hand into a beautifully colored magical gemstone.

In Victorian times chrysoberyls, which count among the most outstanding blooms of the gemstone garden, were generally highly prized, but today they have unfortunately lost their appropriate popularity. Alexandrite is considered as the month stone for June, together with pearl and moonstone.

Garnet and Its Paladins

THE collective name garnet embraces a large mineral group whose members each have their own individual names corresponding to their appearance. This family provides a good example of the fact that though the structure of a mineral determines its external form (garnets crystallize throughout in the cubic system), it is the chemical composition which is fundamental to the color, in that one important component may replace another and in this way produce varieties completely different from one another.

Pyrope, endowed with its glowing red color by allochromatic chromium, is a magnesium-alumina garnet [$Mg_3Al_2(SiO_4)_3$], whose occurrences are confined to Bohemia, South Africa, and Arizona. As a typical representative of basic mineral development, it is formed along with diamond, so that it often provides gem prospectors with a pointer to deeper lying diamond grounds. Bohemian pyropes were much coveted by our forefathers, and beautiful specimens of them decorated the crown jewels of the Bohemian King Wenceslas; for many centuries, because of their slight similarity of color, they were taken for rubies. The always moderating influence of magnesium here ensures the golden mean of properties: the refractive index of pyrope, whose name is borrowed from the Greek word for fire (= pyr), is 1.75, its specific gravity 3.75.

Almandine is a brownish red to reddish violet iron-alumina garnet [$Fe_3Al_2(SiO_4)_3$], colored by the idiochromatic element iron. Wherever iron enters into the chemical composition of a gemstone it deepens the color and heightens the properties. So almandine possesses a higher refractive index (1.795) and greater specific gravity (4.1) than pyrope. Almandines result from various rock-forming processes. They are minerals of igneous and contact-metamorphic rocks as well as of crystalline schists, which explains their wide distribution in almost all important gemstone localities. From the town of Alabanda in Asia Minor Pliny derived the description *carbunculus alabandicus*, which gave almandine its name in the familiar company of the carbuncle stones.

Rhodolite is seen as the link member between pyrope and almandine, with which it forms the red garnet series of the pyrandines. Magnesium and iron are here balanced [$(Mg, Fe)_3Al_2(SiO_4)_3$] and bestow on it the, at present, particularly popular rose-red color and strong luster. The most outstanding rhodolites come from North Carolina, and from Africa's new treasure chest, Tanzania.

In spessartite, a manganese-alumina garnet [$Mn_3Al_2(SiO_4)_3$], another surprising member joins the family; its hot orange hue embodies the molten fires of the earth's core,

40 Garnet is one of the oldest-known gemstones, but
it still surprises us with new occurrences and colors.

and, when large and clear and cut with many facets, it is one of the most outstanding garnets. The combination of manganese with alumina and silica in its composition accounts for its extraordinarily gorgeous idiochromatic color; also for the strongly increased values of light refraction (1.8), thus bestowing a dazzling brilliance on this glowing gemstone, and for the specific gravity (4.16), which considerably reduces the labor of separating it out from alluvial deposits. In Tanzania spessartite is recovered, with rhodolite, from a hornblende-gneiss, and in Ceylon, accompanied by essonite, from the gem gravels.

41 Steplike mine producing garnet and corundum from secondary detrital sediments of the Umba River in Tanzania.

42 Separating jig with sieve boxes for recovery of garnets and corundum from the Umba River in Tanzania.

The most unusual among the garnets is certainly the glistening green demantoid, which consists of the combination $[Ca_3Fe_2(SiO_4)_3]$. The rare pigment chromium, as well as an amazingly high refractive index (1.89) and its fire (0.057) exceeding that of diamond, wreathes demantoid in its aureole of coruscating beauty, which might seriously rival even emerald were demantoid not softer and so extremely rare that it is found in only two places, the Congo and the Urals.

The appearance of grossularite, a calcium-alumina garnet $[Ca_3Al_2(SiO_4)_3]$, is less splendid but at the same time more varied. The most familiar is the brown to dull red-brown essonite (cinnamon stone) from Ceylon and Brazil, to which has recently been added a clear sparkling copper-gold variety from Quebec in Canada and a light green from Tanzania. Both the brothers from the Transvaal—the gooseberry green massive grossularite dotted with black spots and the raspberry red massive grossularite—are opaque.

The origin of the name "garnet," from Latin *granatus* = seed, refers to the appearance of very tiny crystals, usually unsuited for gem purposes, thickly sprinkled in matrix, as they occur in the most striking deposit in mica schists beneath the Manhattan area of New York city. Garnet is regarded as the protector of the crusader from wounds and poison, and as the birthstone for those born in January, symbolizing fidelity, friendship, and constancy.

Moonstone: Child of the Dawning Day

FOR the first time we encounter in this delicate, virginal gem, a gemstone from the ranks of the rock-forming feldspars. Taken all together as a group, the feldspars are the most widely distributed mineral association. Their chemical composition divides them into three different combinations of calcium, sodium, and potassium coupled with alumina and silica, all of which may mutually displace one another. Moonstone constitutes their most important and most valuable variety. The island of Ceylon, treasure house of the world, yields the most charming examples in colors from crystallized veils of mist alternating between soft gray and spring clear, shimmering silvery white. In the southwest of the island in Weeragoda near Ambalangoda they are dug from secondary sediments of aluminous soil, and also mined as primary constituents of pegmatitic veins with quartz as accessory material. In the Moonstone Temple of Anuradhapura, according to tradition, the altar steps were faced with mosaics of exquisite shimmering moonstones. The ruins of this dagoba, built about 1100 B.C., can still be seen. In recent years moonstones of Indian origin have also become known. New workings in the district of Kangyam in the south of India have brought to light, amongst others, moonstones with cat's-eye effects or four-rayed stars. Their colors vary from brown to reddish-brown, leaden gray to black; sporadically, yellow and pink-tinted hues crop up. Cut into artistic cameos they are in high favor, especially in America. Smaller deposits of moonstones are found near Mogok in Burma, also in Brazil, in Australia, and in several places in North America. Moonstone is not a homogeneous mineral but is made up of microscopically fine lamellae composed alternately of the potash feldspar orthoclase and the sodium feldspar albite. The low specific gravity (2.56) of most feldspars falls to its lot, and a low refractive index (1.52), which does not vie with the subtle schiller. The lamellar structure gives rise, through the diffusion of incident light, to the much prized blue shimmer which, as the stone is moved, darts across its convex surface. This lovely phenomenon is called adularescence, from the mineralogical name "adularia" taken by moonstone from its former classic place of origin, the Adula (Rheinwaldhorn) in Switzerland. From ancient times men have considered it the favorite of the moon. At full moon, placed beneath the tongues of lovers, it is said to awaken tender passions. Thanks to its light, bright colors, the moonstone—birthstone of June—endows its protégés with faith in happiness and good fortune.

43 Whether blue, white, green, or orange, moonstone
always entrances all young people with its lovely shimmer.

Opal: the Patchwork Harlequin

In precious opal the earth has given us another gemstone whose magic beauty—a fascinating play of sparkling colors—does not depend on included coloring agents but on an intriguing effect of light. Through diffraction of the incident light by ultramicroscopically fine grating planes within the stone, it is split into its spectral colors, clothing the opal in its iridescent rainbow mantle. It is the only gemstone described in this book which lacks an orderly atomic lattice and which, consequently, is not crystalline. It has, rather, a jellylike structure, not bounded at its periphery by any geometrically definable form. Such substances are called amorphous, which means formless. Built into its ground mass of amorphous silica are serried rows of myriads of the most minute siliceous spherulites composed of shell-like concentric layers of radiating fibers. These tiny spheres are more or less regularly joined together into discrete network layers or network blocks, which make ideal diffraction gratings. The diameter of the spherulites measures less than 0.0005 millimeters. Under the electron microscope they resemble well-packed miniature ping-pong balls. The little spheres, arranged in gridlike fashion, and the spaces between them, approximately correspond in their dimensions to the wavelengths of visible light, which, on striking the grid of spheres, is diffracted and thus split up into its prismatic colors. Size, pattern, and distribution of the flecks of color are determined by the precision and extent of the arrangement in rows, but the diffracted colors of the individual patches are caused by the volume, that is, the number of shells making up the minute spheres. The more uniform the packing of the individual silica bodies and the more regular their distribution according to size, the more brilliant and vibrant is the fleeting play of color. In precious opal extensive planes of gridlike, accurately aligned rows of homogeneously large spheres run through the glassy body of the stone and create an authentic diffraction grating.

The origin of the structure evoking this beautiful effect is related to the process which formed the opal mass. In the volcanic deposits of Honduras, Nevada (deposits in volcanic ash beds), Idaho, Mexico, and Hungary, the nascent substance was composed originally of an aggregate of calcite grains which filled cavities and veins in lava rocks. In the last period of rock formation, hot watery brines rose from volcanic magmas or nearby thermal springs, carrying jellylike silica in solution; this displaced the calcite fillings and in their place injected a mixture of colloidal silica and water ($SiO_2 + nH_2O$), which later

74

44 No other gemstone radiates such dazzling sheaves of gorgeous spectrum
colors as opal, which has recently come into high favor once again.

became opal. Particularly good examples of this silicification process are provided by the Mexican and Hungarian opal occurrences.

In Australia, the main producer today of fantastic fiery, flaming black opal, the opal occurrences are found in fine-grained clayey sedimentary rocks and coarse-grained conglomerate beds, which consolidated during the Cretaceous Period (from 65 to 135 million years ago). The process of silica precipitation, which began in the early Tertiary, i.e. in the last 70 million years, required eons of time. Out of the sediments being eroded, subterranean streams and groundwater flows leached silica, transporting it with them until they came to rest in cracks or depressions. Here the silica collected in the ground where, under the transforming effect of renewed concentration and water evaporation, it was gradually converted into opal. To have produced a piece of opal weighing 5 pounds, 5 tons of water must have evaporated. The different body colors of opal (white, gray, blue, green, orange, and black are known) vary with the chemical differences of the sedimentary rocks or with the trace elements iron, cobalt, copper, nickel, silver, and so on with which the opal was contaminated from the country rocks.

The recovery of opal is arduous labor and a game of luck, only undertaken by a few individual prospectors or small groups of opal hunters. In desolate, sun-scorched deserts, where scanty bushes offer no protection from the harsh, burning rays of the sun and no streams flow, these hardy diggers search for the precious gem. Gouging techniques and exploitation methods seem to be the same throughout all the Australian opal fields. The opal-bearing seams and cavity fillings lie in sedimentary rocks at depths of from 5 to 40 meters beneath the surface. The opal gouger digs with primitive tools a shaft from 4 to 25 meters in diameter and deepens it until he meets the opal horizon. From here he drives tunnels in different directions into the surrounding rock, following the opal seams of only a few centimeters' thickness. Many a gouger has in this way destroyed a fortune by shattering, unawares, a concealed cavity filling of valuable opal. When production becomes uncertain, or the over-deep shaft threatens to cave in, the miner abandons it to try his luck once again in the same manner at another place.

A few years ago a hitherto unknown and unusually interesting occurrence was discovered in Tanzania supplying green, so-called prase, opal, which owes its color to a small nickel content derived from weathered serpentine. Since the opal here, as in all the other localities, crops out relatively near the earth's surface in fairly easily workable rocks, it is merely quarried out by human muscle power with crowbars or picks, and then broken up into smaller pieces with a rock hammer.

Wherever opal occurs it is universally a secondary mineral—that is, deposited in the rocks long after they were formed—in contrast to the majority of other gemstones which crystallized out at the same time as the rock consolidated. This explains why opal occurrences are never found at great depths and do not attain a high geological age. For the same reason opals are never found in alluvial gem gravels but are everywhere mined

45 At Hanety Hill in Tanzania a native miner
breaks up opal-bearing rock in a small quarry.

46 A seam of green prase opal cuts through brown
jasperized serpentine rock at the Hanety Hill in Tanzania.

solely from their primary matrix rocks. Opal is, consequently in no need of high specific
gravity (2.0) which, in secondary deposits, would help it to sink into concentrated
pockets. It can do without the high optical properties of other gemstones; its refractive
index, at 1.45, is little higher than that of water (1.30); if it were higher, it would only
impair its harmonious play of flaming color.

Thus every gemstone, through Nature's wise foresight, was given the requisite
properties to make it some day a jewel for mankind.

The story of opal's origin, like its name—from the Sanskrit word *upala* = precious
stone—turns one's thoughts to India. There, endless ages ago, the Eternal changed a
glamorous woman, wooed by three gods, into a phantom cloud, in order to check their
jealous rivalry. So that they might recognize the bewitched beauty, Brahma sent her his
heavenly blue, Vishnu the sun's golden light, and Siva his fiery red. The Eternal therefore
granted the phantom a new form, of striking appearance, as opal. Pliny wrote that opal

was the goblet of union from which the carbuncle had drunk its smoldering glow, the amethyst its deep purple, the emerald its joyous sea green, the topaz its golden yellow, and the sapphire its deep blue.

In order to define the difference between the various waxing and waning patterns of fire, they are labelled mosaic, flash, and pin-fire. Among them the design of the valuable harlequin opal occupies a coveted, unique position, with its entire surface divided up into a checkerboard pattern, from which, with changing incidence of light, each of the colored squares sparkles into a new fiery color. It seems almost incredible that an orange-red gemstone of clear transparency is also numbered among the opals. This is the fire opal, tinted by iron in graded reddish hues, the best specimens of which blaze in purest orange, but lack the changing, spontaneous play of color of the precious opal.

Prized by orientals since time immemorial as the "anchor of hope" and symbol of purity, whose wearer is held in the hand of God and has nothing to fear from illness, the opal fell into disfavor in the Western world as a victim of superstition. Even today one hears the notorious words "Opals bring bad luck." But rational people will not allow themselves to be influenced in the slightest degree by the alleged magic powers of a gemstone; on the contrary, they are wholeheartedly enchanted by the darting colored lightning and iridescent beauty of opals. These flickering flashes of color from a petrified rainbow induced in the people of past centuries a shiver of awe, as indicated in the romantic novel *Anne of Geierstein* by Sir Walter Scott, when the heroine's maid recounts the superstitious legends (later factually explained) surrounding the opal handed down to the former by her Persian grandmother. The foolish desire to classify gemstones into good and evil was thus stirred up again. Being wiser, the Romans considered the so-called opthalmos (from the Greek ophthalmos = the eye) stone as a universal remedy against eye diseases as well as a good luck charm, withal, and an infant Cupid, a "child lovely as love," as they prettily named it. For Mark Anthony, too, a costly opal ring became the proof of his love for Cleopatra. But the owner of the opal as large as a hazelnut, the Roman Senator Nonius, preferred to go into exile rather than part with it. The well-known Hungarian opals in the crown jewels of the Viennese Hofburg, where the Belgian Princess Stephanie's extensive set of opal jewelry may be seen—girdle, bracelets, earrings, hairpins, necklaces—were no less famous than the ten bangles in Queen Victoria's choice collection. As ruler of the British Empire, to which Australia with its incomparable black opals belonged, she had access to the most precious stones. Not only did she in her time have the British crown jewels embellished with her favorite stone, but she also gave luxurious opal jewelry to her daughters and granddaughters in their turn.

No other gemstone sets ablaze, as opal does, the splendor of the entire color spectrum of the other precious stones—the glowing red of ruby, the soothing green of emerald, the meditative blue of sapphire, and the scintillating gold of yellow diamond—in such a twinkling, colorful ballet suite.

Peridot: Stone of the Heavens

THE beguiling luster of this attractive gemstone—shining like damp moss in autumn sunshine—earned peridot the sobriquet of "green gold." In earlier times it was readily linked with the sun, of whose bright rays it was said to be the keeper and therefore alleged to be a shield against the threat of eclipse and blindness of the eyes. Peridot belongs to the olivine family, whose aristocratic representative it is. Here we meet a second gemstone, like garnet, which is a member of an isomorphous series of mixed crystals. By this is understood the property of interchanging inherent elements without altering the crystal structure. Peridot stands approximately in the middle of such a series, flanked by two unprepossessing minerals as end members. The iron content is critical, since it belongs as the idiochromatic coloring agent in the chemical composition. It is a magnesium iron silicate $[(Mg, Fe)_2SiO_4]$, in which magnesium and iron are combined with silica in varying proportions. At the low-iron end of the mixture series stands the colorless forsterite and at the iron-rich end the black fayalite. Peridot therefore acts as the central link member of the olivines which, although they are very important rock-forming minerals of the basic magmas of the sima, only attain gem quality in rare cases.

Peridot is an early crystallization, formed during the solidification of igneous rocks in the liquid magmatic phase. As a microscopically small crystallite, it even participated decisively in the formation of diamonds. In kimberlite, its ultimate mother rock, peridot is a constituent component, which, in the primary diamond deposits of South Africa, is also responsible for the bluish-green color of the "blue ground."

On the barren desert island of Zebirget (St. John) in the Red Sea, the former classical source of peridot, it is embedded in a plutonic rock called gabbro, which crystallized extremely slowly from great molten masses in the depths of the earth. Thus very large and undisturbed crystals were able to develop, which were typical of Zebirget and for which the island was famed for thousands of years. In fact, peridot is one of mankind's long familiar gemstones. Even 1500 years before the birth of Christ it was hewn by Egyptian slaves out of its dark matrix on the little island; the ancient Egyptians, who knew it under the name of *topazion*, prized it especially as a jewel stone, used mainly for ear pendants.

The island, often enveloped in mist, was difficult of access, whence sailors named it *topazion*, derived from the Greek verb "to seek." For centuries it bore the simple name topaz, until slowly the French name peridot (which comes from the Arabic word *faridat*

47 Peridot, with its superb olive green hue, is found much
less often in large crystals than in small fragments and grains.

= gemstone) superseded it. The magnificently shaped crystals were first brought by the Crusaders to Central Europe, where their special suitability for sacred purposes was soon recognized. Indeed, in the church history of medieval times, when it was used to decorate altars, it was almost indispensable.

In Hawaii peridot is interspersed in a fine-grained, massive basalt, from whose dark groundmass the olive green crystals stand out clearly. Recovery is not possible from the basalt itself owing to the great hardness of the rock. Moreover, the average size of the crystals amounts to only a few carats. Near Hilo in Hawaii, however, small peridots are also found in a secondary deposit of fine black sand, derived from the basalt. These stones, too, are small but, thanks to the natural sorting process, mostly good cuttable specimens have been preserved.

After Hawaii, which strews its peridot carelessly as green grains on the sandy shore, the most prolific source today is found a few kilometers north of Mogok, the legendary valley of rubies in Burma, on the north slope of the 2,250-meter high mountain Kyaukpon. In contrast to rubies, sapphires, spinels, and many other gemstones with which the Mogok valley has blessed us, peridot is not found in gem gravels. It crops out sprinkled as small- to medium-sized shining green crystals in a loose, weathered greenish serpentine resulting from the metamorphism of a ferruginous gabbro. Like glimmering owl's eyes, bright well-shaped crystals of peridot blink here and there from the hydrated serpentine. The probably hydrothermal metamorphism of the former plutonic rock altered only the mother rock without attacking the large gem quality crystals, richer in magnesium. So the clear, green peridots have lain safely for millions of years, cradled in their rock womb, whose relative plasticity has shielded them from seismic blows of fate, until men discovered them and hoisted them from the darkness of their dens into the golden sunlight. Mining in the soft serpentine is comparatively easy and it is sufficient to blast quarries out of the mountain flank or to sink shafts. The rock fragments are then reduced with stone hammers and the peridot crystals, which may weigh up to 100 carats, are thus released and collected up into baskets by hand.

A decidedly unique source of "precious olivine" was discovered in the year 1749 in the east Siberian province of Yenisei. Perfect cuttable crystals were found in a large meteorite, named the Krasnoyarsk Meteorite after the provincial capital. This was the more remarkable because, while other gemstones also do literally fall from the heavens, though they are always tiny, peridot is not even common on earth. Shortly after the Second World War its distribution shrank even more. A gemstone variety closely related to it, and for a long time regarded as peridot, was proved to be a mineral in its own right. Because of its sole occurrence in Ceylon, it was named sinhalite in reference to the old Sinhalese name of its home, Sinhala.

The delightful appearance of peridot and its piquant attraction dubbed it the premier gemstone of the Baroque era, and made its green the hallmark of the age; for its lovely color admirably suited the mentality and decorative schemes of that stylistic epoch. The golden olive green, with its slightly oily glaze, was and is a favorite of gracious beauty and glittering luster. A peridot of 192 carats' weight, crystal clear and of an exquisite olive green, is believed to have been formerly part of the Russian Czarist insignia. Because of its summer-fresh green, peridot is regarded as the birthstone for the month of August. Mounted in gold and worn on the left hand, it is said to put ghosts and demons to flight, dispel melancholy and foolishness, and to show the eternal paths to wisdom.

48 The laboriously won peridots are hauled up out of deep mines on perilously swaying, fragile bamboo scaffolds. Kyaukpon near Mogok, Burma.

Quartz: Jack of All Trades

ON all continents, in the sand of the seashore, in fissures in the Alps—everywhere quartz is to be found, the most ubiquitous mineral on our earth. The reason for this is that silicon dioxide (SiO_2) penetrated throughout the entire magmatic cycle and participated, as quartz, in all stages of rock and mineral formation. In gem quality, with a series of attractive varieties, it emanated only from the pegmatitic, and principally from the hydrothermal, phase. The most valuable specimens are obtained from primary sources, for any quartz lying in gem gravels is washed out during sieving, with the unusable spoil, because of its low specific gravity of 2.65. Its low refractive index of only 1.545 demands as richly faceted a cut as possible, in order to enhance its brilliance by an active play of light.

Water-clear rock crystal handed the euphonious name crystal down to us from the golden age of ancient Greece. The Hellenes believed that the *krystallos* from the mountains was ice turned to rock, from which the gods had built an earthly dwelling impervious to the heat of the sun. Like the smoky gray, and brown to almost black smoky quartz, the far more valuable variety of amethyst (from the Greek *amethyein* = to be immune from drunkenness) also gained its lilac to deep violet color not only from allochromatic pigments but also from the age-long incidence of extraterrestrial cosmic radiation. Its color is consequently often unstable and subject to change on heating. The best-known evidence of such thermal color change is the yellow to reddish-brown citrine, which unfortunately is widely offered for sale under the usurped name topaz. In the natural state citrine exists only as a very light yellow gemstone. In the deposits of the north Brazilian state of Bahia amethysts occur in cavities very similar to the alpine fissures. In Minas Gerais they are found in pegmatites in company with smoky quartz. In both the occurrences in Rio Grande do Sul (south Brazil) and near Catalan in adjacent Uruguay they form drusy linings in agate amygdules which have developed in the magmatic rocks. Compared with these classic sources, all others are insignificant. As the birthstone for those born in February, amethyst is linked with durability and steadfastness in love, calling, and friendship. The church has always bestowed on it, even to the present day, a priestly and even hallowed character.

49 Quartz is a gregarious mineral, and, in addition to rock crystal, presents
us with amethyst, morion (smoky quartz), praseolite, rose quartz, and citrine.

Spinel: Herald of the Princely Corundums

IN her magic garden of crystal blossoms deep in the earth, the Earth Goddess cherished a treasure of choicest excellence, to which she gave an abundance of melting colors, as well as high refraction (1.72) and vivid fire (0.021), notable hardness (8) and complete absence of cleavage. From the sum of this generous endowment emanated the sprightly spinel, which possibly owes its name to the Greek *spinther*, meaning "spark." The Latin word *spina* means "thorn," so that an alternative derivation of the name spinel from its pointed crystal habit may also spring to mind. However that may be, one is amply justified in considering spinel as an ideal gemstone in its own right, as are corundum and chrysoberyl, for like them, it possesses the most desirable properties: high refractive index, lively "fire," and resistant hardness. Of some rarity—especially in good, clear specimens of over 10 carats—spinel commands a retinue of most striking multicolored varieties, which rival the corundum, beryl, and tourmaline species in almost all hues. In past centuries spinel was often confused with the similar-looking corundums—rubies and sapphires; but today, when the advanced state of science enables subtle distinctions to be made, its resemblance to precious ruby and sapphire is no longer an advantage. In olden times its luxurious diversity of colors permitted spinel's admission, under false names, into regalia. The spinel best known in this way is the legendary so-called Timur Ruby, a ruby-red spinel of 361 carats, whose adventurous travels can be traced back to the fourteenth century, when it was stolen in Delhi by the Turcoman-Mongolian conqueror Timur (Tamerlane, 1336–1405). Since 1612 it has shared the same fate as the large Koh-i-noor diamond, since both have always belonged to the same owner. It is remarkable, too, how many owners they have both had. Together they have dwelt in India, in Persia, in Afghanistan, and now they embellish the British Crown Jewels. Around 1850 the East India Company acquired it from the King of Lahore—still with the Koh-i-noor—in order to present it to Queen Victoria of Great Britain. Since then this splendid spinel, flanked by two rubies, has formed the centerpiece of a diamond-set necklace. Another famous ruby-red spinel appears in historical chronicles under the name of The Black Prince's Ruby. It was a gift from Don Pedro the Cruel to The Black Prince of England. Don Pedro, King of Castile in the fourteenth century, had received information that Abu Said, the Moorish ruler of the kingdom of Granada, possessed an

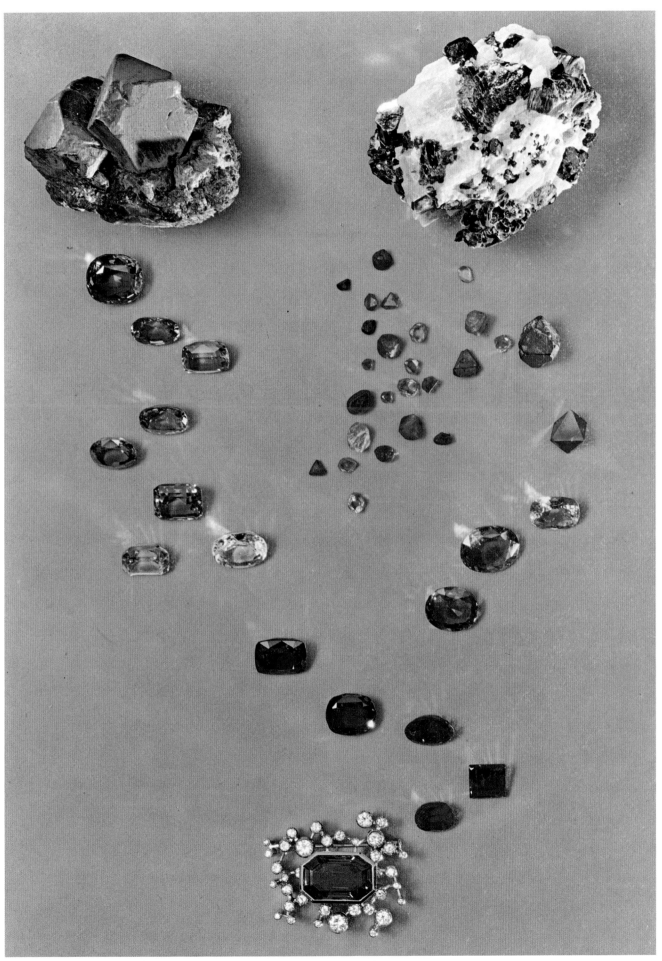

50 Spinel only very rarely develops large crystals, which grow preferentially
as octahedra, but the range of colors and shades is all the more sumptuous.

51 Simple washing plant at a spinel mine near Mogok, Burma.

unusually large and beautiful ruby. So greedily did Don Pedro covet this gem that he stopped at nothing to have it brought to him. Unsuspectingly Abu Said accepted Don Pedro's invitation and appeared at the royal court with great splendor, where he and his train were treacherously struck down. Don Pedro was not permitted to enjoy his stolen goods for long; when he was defeated in battle by his half-brother Henry of Transtamar, he lost his kingdom and fled to Bordeaux to the Black Prince, who was at that time Duke of Aquitaine. The fugitive succeeded in winning over his host to his own cause. As a token of gratitude for the assistance in arms and the victory won near Najera (1367), he gave the precious stone to the Black Prince. After the Prince's death the coveted gem was inherited by the tragic Richard II, and doubtless fell into Bolingbroke's possession when he ascended the throne as Henry IV: the lovely stone is heard of again at the Battle of Agincourt, where King Henry V wore it in his golden helmet. In Cromwell's inventory of the Crown Jewels it is described as a "large balas ruby" and assigned a value of a whole 4 pounds! Today this magnificent ruby-red spinel, set in a Maltese cross of brilliant-cut diamonds, surmounts the Imperial State Crown, and year by year is admired by thousands in the Tower of London. The stone most probably came from Burma; it has never been cut and was nearly 5 centimeters across when last measured. The largest spinel known hitherto, a waterworn crystal of 520 carats, is in the Mineral Department of the British Museum (Natural History), together with a well-formed octahedron of 355 carats; a third giant, of nearly 400 carats, lies in the Diamond Treasury in Moscow.

Nature has endowed every gemstone with characteristics of the most individual kind. In addition to its high aesthetic value, especially its vibrant colors and striking clarity, spinel has still other enhancing qualities, such as its excellent "cuttability" and its capacity

52 Near Mogok in Burma whole families are employed in washing gemstones, of which spinels form the main harvest.

53 A *kanesema* (gem-washing girl) puddling gemstones
in the tailing channel from a processing installation.

to withstand great heat without change. For all this wealth of virtues, it is a most regrettable fact that spinel is at present not accorded its due recognition; for the fine red and blue spinels, though they are poor relations of ruby and sapphire, nevertheless occupy a distinguished rank among gemstones. The gay variety of colors results from its cheerful willingness to exchange hereditary components for foreign coloring elements. Thus small quantities of chromium, in the order of about 1 to 2 percent, may displace aluminium and in this way give rise to the red hue. Red spinel is in fact the only gemstone which can even approximately rival the red ruby. With unexpected diversity it spans all degrees of the red scale and even glows in blood red, brick red, as well as rose-red guise, to which the bright orange-colored fire spinel is added as a pretty variant. In wonderful color gradations the purple spinel shades over into blue-green and ink-tinted nuances of the blue varieties, of which the extremely rare pure deep blue rates the highest value. Iron, titanium, or zinc (gahnite) are responsible for these shades of color when they displace small percentages of magnesium in the spinel composition. Violet spinels are common; distinctly green ones, in which iron replaces a little aluminium, are virtually unknown, and yellow ones do not occur. What spinel lacks in the color saturation of ruby and sapphire, it makes up by dint of its clear transparency and its brilliance, often enhanced by flawless purity. But this does not mean that all spinels are blessed with absolute purity; on the contrary, in many spinels characteristic inclusions occur as welcome identification marks. Indeed, even in this sphere the spinel seeks to rival corundum, in that occasionally its body is interspersed by a fine silky network of needles of rutile or sphene, whence an alternating play of four- and six-rayed stars is induced upon its convex surface.

Spinel is a combination of magnesia (MgO) and alumina (Al_2O_3) and thus a magnesium aluminate ($MgAl_2O_3$). It crystallizes in sharply defined octahedra. It often shares with corundum the same places of origin, mainly in Burma where it is universally accompanied by ruby, and in Thailand, where it is regarded as a "pilot mineral" of corundum. Further important spinel deposits exist in Ceylon. Both spinel and corundum originate from the same pegmatitic-pneumatolytic contact metamorphism. Spinel was, as it were, the herald of the subsequent ruby, crystallizing out in the generation before ruby, in fact, so long as the magnesium dissolved out of the dolomitic limestone was still available. Because of this—in the course of the crystallization processes in which the several mineral generations were involved, magnesia and alumina were continuously consumed—the magnesia was finally used up in the spinel, and only very little alumina was left. This is one explanation why, for example, near Mogok about five times more spinels are found than rubies, and why ruby becomes so extremely rare because the raw material has been exhausted in the spinel. But the image of spinel as the herald of corundum survives even in our day, for it is willingly purchased by every gem fancier who cannot or not yet afford a ruby or a sapphire. The lovely colors of spinels and their strong brilliance will always gladden the heart of a gemstone lover.

Topaz: Captive Gold of the Sun

EVER since man became acquainted with topaz, this noble stone has been paying dearly for the melodiousness of its name, which was formerly bestowed on the whole range of all yellow to golden brown gemstones. At the heart of such misnomers is the citrine, a variety of quartz mostly obtained through the heating of amethyst. This stone, lacking brilliance and fire, with its glassy luster, is not only far removed from, but not even worthy to be compared with, the incomparably more lively, more brilliant topaz, flaunting its warm golden tones. The glowing, fiery sparkle of topaz has always enchanted poets and men of taste with its beguiling resemblance to the flaming splendor of a noble wine. As a result of the poet's words, the popular mind is imprinted with an image of topaz only as beautiful clear golden drops; in this way, however, other knowledge has been lost, namely, recognition of the wide scale of the blue shades and delicate pink tones of topaz, which are of equally enchanting intensity and strong luster. The range of glittering pink topazes spans all stages of rose shades, culminating in an incomparable full and saturated rose-red which, in its flaring brilliance, even surpasses the exquisite morganite of the beryl family. As the golden topaz is indebted for its rich sunny tone to a harmonious blending in of peach-pink, so a hardly discernible neon-blue shimmers through the reddish specimens. The blue topaz bathes the eye with its fresh, shining azure blue, without ever reaching the deep saturation of the aquamarine. Of perfectly pure color, without the slightest addition of green, it presents a maidenly charm as its gradually diminishing color passes into colorless to pure white topaz. This, too, formerly caused some confusion. Thus, the Braganza Diamond of 1,680 carats in the Portuguese Crown Jewels is in fact a colorless topaz, while, on the contrary, a "topaz" half as big as a pigeon's egg in a peasant jewel from the lower Rhine was recognized about 1929 as a yellow diamond.

The rarest are the pink-colored topazes, which, in their loveliest guise of sparkling *vin-rosé* color, are native to the Urals. Since the Bolshevik October Revolution no precious stones have been exported thence—at least until recent times no gemstone deposits have been mined there. Somewhat lighter but of the purest cherry-blossom pink are the pink topazes from Brazil. In this country, too, their decided rarity holds good. Most of the pink topazes seen in the trade are heat-treated ones originally golden in color. For this purpose stones are chosen whose golden color, as a result of an unattractive reddish tinge, demands enhancement.

Topaz, crystallizing in the rhombic system, develops prisms with rectangular or

54 Topaz, a typical pegmatite mineral, likes to grow on quartz, and often develops into large crystals. It furnishes clear enchanting gemstones in delicate shades of yellow, brown, pink to wine red and light blue.

55 Topaz concentration in a pegmatite vein of feldspar and quartz near Dom Bosco in the neighborhood of Ouro Preto-Belo Horizonte in the state of Minas Gerais, Brazil.

lozenge-shaped basal planes, as well as many-faced terminations, and—thanks to its good gem hardness—takes an excellent polish. The extreme smoothness of its surface even provides a diagnostic property; for, as well as by its characteristic colors, it may easily be distinguished in the hand from other similar gemstones by its slippery touch. The considerably higher refractive index (1.62) gives topaz the advantage of superior brilliance over the pretentious citrine. In addition to this, a simple means of distinction offers itself to the gemmologist in the methylene iodide test. With a specific gravity of 3.33 this solution separates the two rivals, in that the lighter citrine (2.65) floats, while the heavier topaz (3.53–3.56) sinks to the bottom. Even together, the Urals, Burma, Ceylon, and the United States cannot compete with that classic crucible of pegmatites in Brazil—the gem-rich state of Minas Gerais—which shelters under its weathered dome the choicest topazes both in quality and quantity; here they are recovered, together with aquamarines, either from their primary source or from the valley floors somewhat downstream. Their great scarcity is explained by the fluorine so vital to their existence—one of the volatile constituents, enriched in the pegmatitic residual magmas, from which the chemical compound

$Al_2(F,OH)_2SiO_4$ results. Where the rare elements, such as beryllium, boron, fluorine, and lithium, providing the key to the genesis of beryl, topaz, and tourmaline, could not move far from their origin within the residual magmas, their compounds are found almost exclusively in pegmatites. Nevertheless, not all topazes grow from pegmatitic mineral formation, for fluorine-rich solutions also impregnated the country rock at an even later stage and, where hot enough, dissolved the existing minerals. Thus silica and alumina were freed so as to combine with the fluorine to form topaz. Such processes of replacement took place mainly in cracks and druses. It is exclusively the topazes from these pneumatolytic-hydrothermal deposits which concern the gem market, for here every glorifying property—beauty of color, hardness, and durability—is imparted to them, elevating them into sought after and treasured gemstones. The variety of the occurrences and of their genesis likewise produces distinguishable features in their crystals, and thus each type of deposit produces its corresponding topaz crystal. Collectors and connoisseurs can, from the appearance of a topaz crystal, recognize from what type of formation and often even from which actual locality it comes. The origin of topaz colors has so far not been as thoroughly investigated as those of other gemstones; nevertheless, the assumption is justified that a different oxidation valence of iron decides whether a topaz turns blue or golden. In pink topaz chromium seems to act as the pigment, for in the emission spectrum a bright chromium line appears. In pegmatitic topazes colorless to blue predominate, also pale yellow, while the products of the pneumatolytic-hydrothermal transition stage exhibit the coveted golden and pink tones. Close parallels may be drawn between the colors of topaz and beryl. However, because of their higher refraction and greater hardness (8), topazes exhibit far more advantageous and ideal gemstone properties than beryls; consequently they should retain the buyer's favor, the more so since their prices slightly hold the balance.

The testimony from antiquity about the name *topazion,* "the Sought-and-Found," leads one to suppose that in olden times it was not our gemstone with the appealing golden tinge which was meant at all, but most probably peridot. For Pliny describes, under the name of topaz, a green gem which has nothing in common with the brownish-yellow tone of the November birthstone, which symbolizes friendship. On the other hand, the peridot from Zebirget Island in the Red Sea flourished for a long time under the name *chrysolite,* which means "golden stone"—a name perhaps better suited to topaz.

The topaz was much prized in the Middle Ages. The majority of the wine-yellow crystals produced during those times were provided by the Schneckenstein in the Erzgebirge mountain range between Saxony and Bohemia. Augustus the Strong of Poland, who is remembered in history as a luxury-loving prince, had many of his splendid court jewels adorned with the topazes so highly prized by him.

Unusually large and, in some cases, very beautiful topazes are owned by the mineralogical museums in Florence, London, Paris, and Vienna.

Tourmaline: The Crystallized Kaleidoscope

ALL stages of imaginable color possibilities are captured by this gemstone which, in addition to white and black, embraces every hue to be found in the spectrum, not only in pure tones but in all the fine nuances of innumerable shades, transitions, and mixtures. Should a collector set himself the task of amassing all the colorings of tourmaline, he would find a lifetime insufficient to incorporate the thousands upon thousands of ever differently tinted specimens into his collection. Mixed colors are an innate feature peculiar to tourmaline. Because of its moderate refractive index (1.64), it eschews striking brilliance in favor of a modest restraint and comforting tranquillity. It contents itself with a soft, mellow, one might almost say tender luster, which in a single stone harmonizes into a lovely color symphony of manifold tones. In this multicoloration, tourmaline displays in masterly fashion the distinctive characteristic of pleochroism (differential selective absorption), which results from the property of absorbing incident light differently in different directions. Through this peculiarity, one and the same individual stone may appear in more than one distinct color. In tourmaline this phenomenon is caused by an interchangeability between divalent and trivalent iron.

But there is no end to the magic of this truly astonishing family of stones; there is still another inherent oddity to be appreciated. Crystallizing trigonally and thus developing three-sided prisms with often very beautiful terminations, tourmaline exhibits within one individual crystal, contrasting colors which once again describe a wide arc from the lightest to the darkest shades. At one end of the crystal we may, for example, find ruby-red rubellite, at the other end sapphire-blue indicolite, and in between, all conceivable notes are sounded from orange, through brown and yellow, to green. The yellow and brown tourmaline colors are caused by trivalent iron, that of the blue by divalent iron.

Wherever magnesium displaces the iron the shades become lighter. Manganese ripens into pink to red colorings; the drowsy hue of green tourmaline, resembling that of magnolia leaves, emanates from chromium or vanadium.

The degree of hardness (7.5) and the specific gravity (3.05) favor the recovery of tourmaline wherever it occurs, be it in Africa, Burma, Ceylon, California, or Madagascar. In Brazil, the most important treasure house of tourmaline, it is found in all colors

56 Tourmaline, clearly a pegmatitic mineral, provides an overwhelming
abundance of colors, which still offer surprises every now and then.

57 Entrance to an exploitation gallery in the primary tourmaline deposit in pegmatite rock near Itambacuri in the state of Minas Gerais, Brazil. Pick and shovel, bucket and basket are, not only in the secondary but also in many places in the primary occurrences, the only scanty tools with which the heavy manual labor of gemstone mining is done. Thus the winning of only a few gemstones involves a huge expenditure of effort.

mentioned above; moreover, these are not even scattered through the country but often concentrated in a single pegmatite vein, even in a single crystal. As a complex borosilicate $[(Na, Ca) (Li, Mg, Fe, Al)_9B_3Si_6(O, OH)_{31}]$, tourmaline is a typical representative of the plutonic rocks, in which are stored the volatile materials vital to its formation. However, only the black tourmalines originate from pegmatitic melts; the gem qualities are of hydrothermal origin. Its matrix today is an extensively weathered rock which can be very easily broken up. The mining methods in Brazil are therefore of the greatest simplicity. Equipped only with pick and shovel, hundreds and sometimes thousands of itinerant prospectors, called *garimpeiros,* mark out a small claim on the gemmiferous terrain and dig either a shaft or a tunnel according to the nature of the deposit. As soon as the gem cavity or the concentration in the gravel is reached, it is more or less completely exploited. If unworked ground still remains in the neighborhood, the garimpeiros take out a new mining license in order to try their luck for the varicolored stones on this as well. Were it not for the abundant cheap labor, Brazil could never be the generous and important producer of gemstones that it is.

The unsurpassed color magic of the *turamali,* as the Sinhalese used to call all brown gemstones occurring in Ceylon, first became known in Holland in the year 1703 as the "ash magnet," so called from its capacity to become electrically polarized when heated and to attract ashes as well as dust particles. The Dutch used it to draw the ash out of their meerschaum pipes. Those born in October rejoice in the bountiful colors of tourmaline, which—as the Muses' stone—is said to speed the writer's flow of thought.

58 Outcropping tourmaline pegmatite in the Serra Itatiaia near Conselheiro Pena in the state of Minas Gerais, Brazil.

Zircon: The Enigmatic Gemstone

NATURE has conferred on zircon several quite outstanding optical properties which furnish brilliant-cut specimens with a particularly striking appearance. High adamantine luster and very vivid fire elevate zircon into the immediate proximity of diamond. Its specific gravity is unequalled by any other transparent gemstone. Its high refractive index of 1.95 and powerful color-dispersive ability of 0.038 make it an impressive gemstone, whose fascination is further increased by the remarkable fact that these values are by no means constant, being subject to a certain variability about whose ultimate rules there is still no general understanding. The visible evidence of double refraction so typically distinct in zircon will not escape the notice of the alert observer. It manifests itself in the lack of sharpness of its pavilion edges when the eye looks from the sharp crown edges into the depth of the stone. Many other gemstones also possess this property of splitting the incident light into two different strongly refracted rays, so that everything seen right through these stones appears doubled.

The colors of zircon offer a profusion of scintillating beauty and complement the optical merits in a highly effective way. The pure substance is in itself colorless, as neither the zirconia nor the silica in its chemical composition ($ZrSiO_4$) are in the least color-bearing. It is extremely probable that the zircon colors are not exclusively due to the chromoforous elements present, but also correlate with the content of the radioactive elements uranium and thorium which are included in varying amounts as trace elements. It is the presence of these radioactive atoms which enables the colors of zircon to be altered by heating, whereby the secret of its manifold shades of color is also revealed. The most coveted colors—blue, extremely rare occurrence in nature, and colorless, the gemstone most closely resembling diamond—are such heat-induced varieties: the blue is produced by heating zircon in a vacuum, while firing in a stream of oxygen decolors zircon. The blue zircon enjoyed great favor during the first half of this century; on the other hand, because of its high refraction and strong fire, the colorless variety is often used as a diamond substitute in imitation jewelry. Unfortunately not all artificially colored zircons prove to be color-fast, for under ultraviolet rays or in daylight they may revert to their original colors.

Zircon, which crystallizes in a tetragonal (four-sided) form, has taken part in different gemstone evolutions and at times accompanies acid plutonic rocks as an accessory component, and at times belongs to pegmatites (vein rocks) and to some crystalline schists.

59 The mysterious zircon is attractive less in its wealth of colors, which include
yellow, brown, red, green, as well as blue tones, than in its lively, diamondlike sparkle.

60 Zircon washers buddle the excavated gravel in
a small water hole on a zircon field in Cambodia.

It is thus found in all kinds of rocks and deposits throughout the world; but the richest
occurrences of gem zircon are found in Cambodia, Ceylon, Burma, Thailand, and
Vietnam, and are without exception alluvial placer deposits, from which the zircon is
washed out as a companion mineral of ruby, sapphire, and many other gemstones. The
zircons of Ceylon are outstanding for their particularly gorgeous color range, since the
island, an extraordinarily fecund source of valuable stones, brings to light the whole broad
spectrum of hues, except blue. Burma, in addition to the rare blue, plucks mainly cognac
brown, green, and red varieties from the dazzling bouquet of colors, while the Indochinese
deposits are characterized by yellow, brown, and reddish-brown specimens.

It was zircon which first enabled the age of a gemstone deposit to be determined.
In many zircons, which have a very high thorium or uranium content, the crystalline
atomic structure gradually collapses under the radioactive bombardment into the

61 Former rubber plantation with innumerable mounds thrown up from small zircon mines. Some of them are being excavated and the spoil is being brought up in baskets on a bamboo hoist, while at the edge of other holes the dug soil is being sifted.

amorphous state of an irregular aggregate of zirconia and silica. The zircons then become cloudy and simultaneously take on a green coloration; the physical values drop; the strong double refraction disappears, and a part of the uranium and thorium alters to lead. The quantitative ratio between uranium and thorium on the one hand, and lead on the other, which is today measurable, permits determination of the age of the zircon and hence of its deposit. In this way it has been calculated, for example, that the gem gravels of Ceylon are about 550 million years old. A few years ago the discovery of ekanite, a new radioactive gemstone from Ceylon, enabled the author to confirm these age determinations.

Zircon, with its many features, was in earlier times called "hyacinth." The name is supposedly to be traced back, through intervening oriental stages, to the Greek *hyakinthos*. The more recent name zircon comes from the Persian word *zargun,* which means gold-colored.

The Collector's Viewpoint

OVER and above the gemstones already described there are still numerous minerals which make beautiful gemstones in cut form as well as completely fulfilling the requirements of beauty, rarity, and durability. Their popularity and their market success are mostly determined by their great rarity; because of the latter they are all the more coveted by collectors. Contrary to prevailing ideas, these extremely rare and unusual collectors' delights can be obtained at favorable prices. Together with many others, the varieties pictured on the color plate opposite belong to those gemstones which are most treasured by gemmologists and collectors: From left to right, top row: Yellow amblygonite, an aluminium phosphate containing the volatile elements fluorine and lithium, was discovered in 1953 in a drawer at a mineral museum and recognized as a gemstone in its own right. Asparagus-green andalusite, an aluminous silicate first found in Andalusia, is distinguished by its intense pleochroism which makes the narrow ends appear reddish-brown. As a beryllium aluminium silicate, light green euclase is a close relative of beryl. Lime-green hiddenite and lilac-colored kunzite belong to the spodumene family, an aluminium silicate with a lithium content. Second row: Wine-yellow danburite comes, so far, only from Burma. Yellow-brown sinhalite was first discovered in 1946 in Ceylon. Yellow-orange to brown sphalerite with its leaden luster almost equals the high refraction of diamond. Clear yellow orthoclase, a brother of moonstone, often yields huge specimens from Madagascar. Lively, sparkling phenacite owes its name to its vanity in trying to appear better than it is. The double row in the center displays the rich colors of the fluorite family, whose light green, green, and pink specimens come from Swiss occurrences. Second row from the bottom: Clove-brown axinite crops out in small specimens in the Alps, gem-quality ones in southern California. Apatite, too, is often a mineral of the Alpine clefts. Up to now, the extremely rare sapphire-blue benitoite has been found only in Benito County in California. Yellowish-green brazilianite, so far encountered only in Brazil, has been known only since 1944. Blue cordierite, named in honor of the French geologist P. Cordier, is striking in its strong pleochroism. Bottom row: Pink scapolite from Burma and yellow from Brazil are very popular collectors' stones. But prestige is bestowed upon any gem collection by yellow, green, and brown sphenes which display the most intense fire of all gemstones. Yellow scheelite rivals them in its high refraction of light.

62 The color plate above shows a limited sample of a few particularly beautiful and large specimens of the rarest collectors' gems most sought after by connoisseurs and gemmologists.

Agate: Master of Patterns

THE parade of opaque ornamental stones is led by agate—diversely beautiful, multicolored, and variously formed as it is, its endless abundance of abstract designs can only be hinted at by the descriptions "spotted, cloudy, marbled, banded, or dappled." To the ancient Greeks and Romans it was already known in the form of colored pebbles collected from the Achates River in Sicily. Even the names for its fantastically imaginative pictures—the miniature paintings of tree, dendritic, landscape, moss, and lace agate—are only a modest selection from the inexhaustible wealth of attractive patterns. These dainty pictures, however, have no connection with fossilized plants or other organic residues, but consist of ramifying inclusions of true mineral substances which have crystallized out from ferruginous, manganese-rich, or chloric solutions. The ornamental stones are so-called cryptocrystalline mineral formations (the Greek word *kryptos* meaning "hidden" or "secret"), in whose dense aggregates the microscopically fine crystallites cannot be distinguished individually by the human eye. The agate members of the chalcedony group, which in their turn belong to the quartz family, are descendants of volcanic eruptions, in whose hot molten lavas floated drops of more or less pure silica (SiO_2) with or without water content, in sizes from that of a pea to some weighing a hundredweight. After the lavas solidified into melaphyre rocks the silica crystallized out as radial-fibered quartz masses of roughly almond-shaped form. The rate of crystallization of the silica was governed by the varying rate of cooling, which proceeded by irregular phases. In cyclical layers it precipitated either densely entwined, fine-fibered gray, or porous, coarse-fibered white bands. Such white- and gray-banded agates, whose merit lies in their pronounced capacity to absorb dyes, occur abundantly in the south Brazilian state of Rio Grande do Sul and in the district round Catalan in northern Uruguay. The agates from the United States and from the melaphyre quarries near Idar-Oberstein (Germany) attract special notice by their pretty rose to red, and yellow to brown bands. By "pickling," the porous white agate layers can be dyed. In this way the fine cryptopores between the quartz fibers are filled with, preferably, light-fast metallic coloring agents. By steeping in concentrated sugar solution or honey water, and subsequently treating with sulphuric acid, for example, black and white banded agate can be obtained. Drying and heating ensures the permanence of the colors in all agates dyed in this way: brown to red sand, reddish-brown carnelian, and the so-called layered seal stone or "niccolo."

63 Of all ornamental stones, agate is by far the most ingenious contriver of a
multiplicity of patterns and designs, and is thus always stimulating men to new creations.

Jade: Jewel of Heaven

IN jade is sealed the alliance between man and gemstone through thousands of years. Its use was not confined only to man's ornamental and protective needs in the form of jewelry and amulets, but also served him in the early Stone Age as one of the elementary implements of his culture—as tools for hammering, splitting, and cutting. Although of only moderate hardness (6.5–7), it is of unyielding toughness, and is even capable of denting steel, so that for him it was a weapon in his struggle for existence against raw nature, and later became the preferred cult stone for rendering thanks to the gods. Thus, graves excavated in Mexico have yielded mainly ritual objects of great artistic skill, whence the conclusion may be drawn that *chalchihuitl* (= jadeite) was already held in highest esteem in the blossoming cultures of the Central American Indians.

In the gemstone trade two different minerals fall under the general term "jade," namely, nephrite and jadeite. The ornamental stone nephrite occurs as intercalations in serpentine rocks and in crystalline schists which originated from eruptive rocks low in silica; the same holds true for the jadeite of Burma. Here the acid granitic magma, penetrated by ultrabasic serpentine, suffered a desilication whereby the quartz segregated out and the greater part of the albite ($NaAlSi_3O_8$) was converted into jadeite ($NaAlSi_2O_6$). Wherever chromium happened to be present, the highly prized emerald green Imperial Jade resulted. The precious translucent material is known in numerous delicate colorings. It is usually a soft white ("mutton-fat" jade) with an almost imperceptible pastel hint, and often veined and flecked with emerald green traces of chromic acid, but a stronger concentration of chromium is indicated by the variable green tones, for whose loveliest emerald-green hue enormous sums are paid in the Far East. As a result of tinting by iron, jadeite becomes apple-green to yellowish and on through orange to brown, and, when manganese is present, lavender blue to violet. At restricted localized places the chrome-rich jadeite has been able to color the adjacent albite. After extensive analysis, this shining stone of rice-paddy green, called *maw-sit-sit*, by the local people, was recognized by the author, as an independent ornamental stone in its own right and was named "jade-albite." The color of nephrite is mainly a dark leek to spinach green, and is imparted by iron.

Jade beds are found in many parts of the world, and deposits of some commercial importance occur in North America and New Zealand. But it is to Burma, once again, that the crown is due, the most prolific jadeite mines lying in the northern part of the

64 For hundreds of years jade has been considered as the "gem of heaven"
by the Chinese, whose most precious specimens are artistically carved.

country round Tawmaw and along the precipitous slopes of the Uru River. Among brecciated boulders, in so-called conglomerate accumulations, it is found in geologically recent river deposits relatively close beneath the surface. While the favor of the gods is implored with flowers, paper flags, and fruits, men toil with crowbars, picks, and patient confidence during the six months' dry season from October to April to separate the rare jade blocks from the barren detritus. From Mogaung, where the official inspector submits them to a sun test to ascertain their color and translucency, and estimates their value, most of the stones travel down the Irrawaddy River, through Rangoon, and over the sea to

65 At the foot of the conglomerate hills and deep beneath the alluvium of the Uru River the waterworn jade blocks are today recovered by laborious toil from the bottom of their ancient bed.

66 With marvellous sensitivity to the character and color distribution of the
rough jade, the carver's sure hands create a nobly formed masterpiece of art.

eastern countries. Their destination is Hong Kong where, in small workshops down
twisting alleys, to the continuous accompaniment of pedaling, the masters of jade art carve
their figures on cutting wheels charged with finest diamond dust. Through the handing
down over hundreds of years, experience and skill have reached maturity in these artists.
In classical Chinese art the precious stone *yu* is the earthly embodiment of the cosmic
principle which regulates the spiritual, ethical, and social life in the Middle Kingdom.
Purity, permanence, virtue, and strength inherent in the "jewel of heaven" are given with
awesome care a form subordinated in humility to that granted by Nature: the
proportioned harmony of color and structure as well as their irregularities are incorporated
into the fashioning of the shape, so that everything bestowed by the Creator is used to His
glory. Guided by nothing but intuition and with a sensitive feeling for the nature of each
stone, the carver first of all sketches the envisaged model on the flat stone; then in many
weeks of labor, he shapes a work of art which, by its inherited motifs, continues the living
tradition of his ancestors.

Labradorite and Spectrolite:
Vibrant Rainbows

PURE chance is often the best ally for discovering the secrets of Mother Earth. She surely still holds many surprises in store. Though relevant preliminary studies did effect positive results in this case, it was nevertheless a happy accident for the Finnish mineralogist Laitakari when, during the Russian-Finnish winter campaign of 1939/40 while inspecting fortification emplacements along the border, he climbed up on some granite boulders whose feldspar components exhibited the unmistakable schiller of labradorite. He had thus discovered the Finnish source of a mineral which, until then, had been almost exclusively confined to the Labrador coast of Canada. And not only that, for the new ornamental stone—a variety of labradorite, which is a lime-rich feldspar forming an isomorphous link between $NaAlSi_3O_8$ and $CaAl_2O_8$ and crystallizing in the triclinic system—immeasurably surpasses the hitherto known green- or blue-iridescent specimens in its gorgeous shimmer. Both developed in the liquid-magmatic phase as a primary component of granites. At an appropriate angle to the incident light, manifold intensely dazzling colors suddenly flash out from the dark smoke to ash gray body color: wonderful spectrum colors from blue and green to yellow and orange, through to glowing red, whence the stone has been honored with the name spectrolite. The typical color schiller of labradorite, whose "labradorescence" resembles the iridescent wings of tropical butterflies culminating in the even more complete rainbow colors of spectrolite, changes with the incidence of light. This is caused by the combination of interference and diffraction of light by a microscopically fine grating of the most minute, parallel magnetite needles enclosed in the stone in rigidly controlled alignment and dense succession. Blocks weighing about a ton each are sawn out of the country rock, the granite matrix of the spectrolite, in the neighborhood of Ylijärvi village in Ylämaa parish. As in diamond production, by far the larger part finds industrial application; for in the color-conscious Scandinavian lands the glittering granitic rock, cut into slabs, is in high favor for covering facades and lining walls. The vividly colored fragments used in jewelry are relatively small, but are attractive in their rainbow schiller shown off by flat or curved bands. Because of the small size, it is rarely made into ash trays or figures, but in pendants and cuff links for young people, the shimmering gleam of this captive rainbow is set ablaze by the incident light which alone, as with many other gem or ornamental stones, has the power to awaken its beauty to life.

67 Labradorite, shimmering in blue and green, and spectrolite, gleaming in
its rainbow colors, are precious members of the great feldspar family.

Lapis Lazuli: A Starlit Sky

LAZURITE, as the exquisite royal blue lapis is also called, differs from all other ornamental stones in that it is not a mineral but a rock which—evolving through pneumatolytic alteration from a contact-metamorphosed limestone—is made up of several minerals in varying amounts. As unique as this chemical composition is its unequalled night-dark blue, which Pliny extolled as "a fragment of the starry firmament," and which, long before his time, the ancient Egyptians had already used as inlay in their splendid goldsmiths' work. The name lapis lazuli is based on the Latin *lapis* = stone, and the Arabic *azul* or *al-lazward,* which as well as denoting the sky also includes all nuances of blue. Ancient writings show that this "stone of the sky" has been the preeminent jewel in the land of the Nile for at least 5,000 years for ornamenting bracelets, pendants, daggers and breastplates, and for carving into seal rings, figures, and scarabs. It may be presumed that the Egyptian craftsmen used lapis obtained from Afghanistan, for even today the most valuable material is found in the Firgamu mines in the Badakshan district of the Hindu Kush mountains, where the rock is blasted out of the hillside after being heated and then quenched with cold water. The quality is of an intense ultramarine-blue, evenly colored throughout and flecked with tiny pyrite crystals glittering like metallic gold.

In contrast with this are the less uniformly blue, paler, and—depending on their condition—less costly specimens from the Chilean Andes, which are usually interspersed with calcite intercalations and flecked with white. The incorporated ultramarine molecules of the minerals sodalite, lazurite, and haüynite lend the lapis the warm, particularly attractive blue, whose saturated shade with its imperceptible hint of red made the pulverized lazurite a highly esteemed artist's pigment in the Middle Ages. It also explains its constant popularity since time immemorial for wonderful, carved and inlaid works and for such magnificent objects as the famous lapis lazuli terrestrial globe, made from a single block, on the tomb of Saint Ignatius in Rome, or those regal wall facings which can still be admired in one of the rooms of the small palace town of Tsarskoye-Selo, now known as Pushkin. Whether it is because of its tranquil, well-balanced satin color that it is chosen for elegant necklaces, or because of its mottled and shaded aspect that it is worked into caskets or carved into statuettes, the invigorating blue of lapis is always beguiling to the heart and eye of the beholder.

68 Highly prized in Czarist Russia as a wall facing, lapis
lazuli today finds many varied uses in personal jewelry.

Malachite: Greens Galore!

THE interest of its gnarled banding, which unlike most other ornamental stones is not multicolored but patterned throughout in contrasting shades of light to dark green, has earned malachite many admirers. In ancient times it was likened to the innumerable green shades of mallow leaves. The spirited play of light and dark effects renders it an inexhaustible source of oscillating arched, bent, often twisted, even perfectly circular and concentric lines, curves, and stripes—designs suggesting a bird's-eye view of the boundless primeval forests of its present main supplier, the Congo. The effortless ability to furnish ever-varying patterns whose exquisite harmony can be revealed by means of skillful cutting, originates from the special mode of formation of malachite, which occurs as a surface weathering product from the action of meteoric waters on deeper-lying copper ore lodes. It is a hydrated copper carbonate $[CuCo_3 \cdot CU(OH_2)]$ and thus one of the few stones colored idiochromatically by copper. It is everywhere found in the uppermost horizon of copper ore deposits and forms thick opaque masses composed of tiny monoclinic crystallites. Although malachite, as a mineral, is common, the knolls which are so well suited to cutting, with their rounded, kidney-, grape-, or cone-shaped surface habits, have become rare. The colors, which fluctuate between emerald-green, spinach-green, dark leek-green, and blackish green, together with the alternation of light and dark layers in the concentric shells of its structure, create the magic of its artistic designs. Their charming visual effect is strikingly enhanced by the brilliant silky luster which it acquires on polishing. Extensive strata of large knolls and tabular outcrops in the Urals predestined malachite to become the decorative stone par excellence of Czarist Russia. The columns of the ikonostasis in the world-famous Saint Isaac Cathedral in Leningrad are completely clad with malachite and lapis lazuli; the same applies to the walls of the Malachite Salon in the Winter Palace and the innumerable works of art, tabletops and richly carved vases in the Hermitage. Today malachite is found in scanty and constantly shrinking amounts only in Katanga (Congo), Rhodesia, southwest Africa, and Australia. The glossy green stone with its unusual shell-like patterns was said to make the speech of animals clearly audible. Thanks to its suitability for so many aspects of applied ornamental purposes, for carvings, and for mounting in jewelry, it enjoys great popularity everywhere.

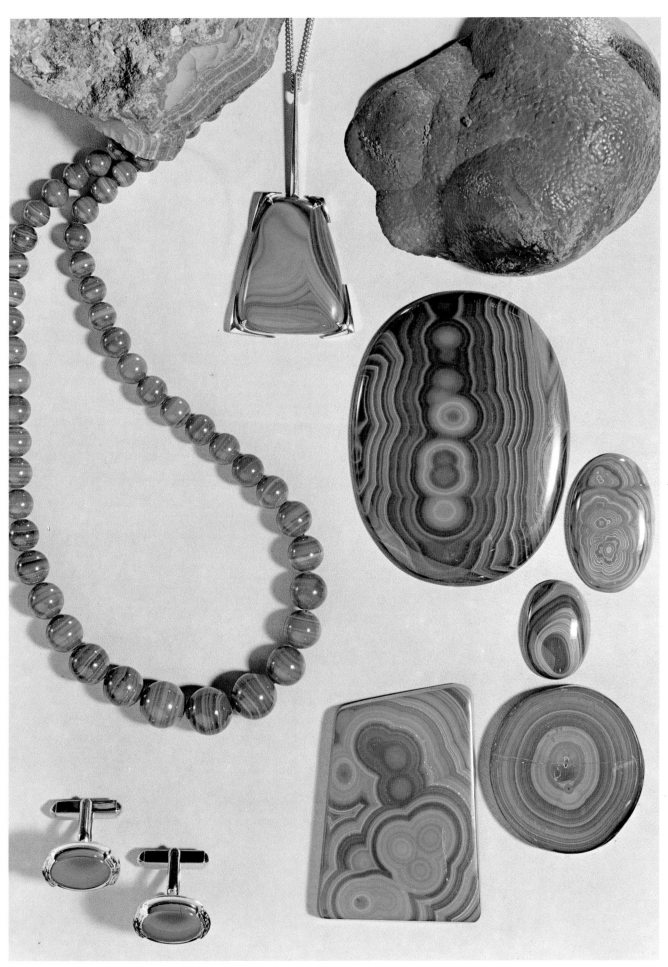

69 Malachite, making imaginative play with shades of mallow
green, has become one of the rarest of ornamental stones.

Rhodochrosite and Rhodonite:
Inca Rose and Peach Blossom

*T*HE display by malachite in its captivating symphony of greens is repeated by rhodochrosite (Greek *rhodon* = rose; *chros* = flesh color) on an equally grand scale in rose-red alternations. The latter is no less prolific in original designs of convoluted banding; with unflagging inventiveness it imprints its patterns in light and dark pink tones. It, too, originates through weathering, of manganiferous limestones. For rhodochrosite is also a carbonate of manganese, $MnCO_3$, occurring in the form of botryoidal or pipelike aggregates, whose individual microscopically tiny stalky crystals possess trigonal symmetry and exhibit the easy cleavage of all carbonates. Known only since the Second World War, rhodochrosite seems little suited to the strenuous demands of daily use in jewelry because of its low hardness. But thanks to its delicate colors it is enjoying increasing favor in handmade handicrafts. The marbled structure of layers, varying from white to glowing raspberry red or dark rose-red nuances, implants unique color compositions and designs on the large surfaces of ashtrays, bowls, or paperweights. The best quality is obtained in San Luis (Argentina) from a silver mine apparently abandoned in the thirteenth century by the Incas, where rhodochrosite has since grown up from the floor toward the roof as stalagmites. This proves that it can be no older than seven hundred years. In recent times the United States has also come to the fore by producing wonderful clear transparent crystals.

Similar to rhodochrosite is the darker, wine-red rhodonite, a manganese silicate $(CaMn_4[Si_5O_{15}])$ with a minor iron and calcium content. The cryptocrystalline aggregates, whose individual units crystallize in the triclinic system, form compact masses with prismatic cleavage. Rhodonite was formerly found in the Urals and was much prized in Russia as a stone both for use in jewelry and for making Easter eggs for gifts. Today Sweden, Australia, California, and Vancouver Island (Canada) are the most important producers of this patrician material. The fine shades of deep rose-red to bluish-red tones and the black veins of manganese oxide together create those animated scenes from which springs the enchantment of this ornamental stone for those endowed with imagination. In the larger oval rhodonite plaque on the bottom of the color plate opposite, for example, a plesiosaur (marine reptile) may be clearly seen in a typical Jurassic landscape—about 150 million years ago—stalking out of a swamp, while above him on a branch an archaeopterix (primitive bird) spreads its wings.

70 Rhodochrosite and rhodonite, two manganese minerals, are gay in charming patterns
and designs brought into being by the graded tones of red, and the black intercalations.

Turquoise: Noontide Sky

THE blue-tinged turquoise can look back upon the same rich and honorable tradition as lapis. While other stones have risen on the horizon of fashion and faded away again, turquoise has retained its favor unharmed over thousands of years. Egypt's Pharaohs already venerated the captivating beauty of its lustrous blue to greenish-blue color four thousand years before the Christian era, when they mined the unattractive raw material in the Sinai peninsula for their lavish jewelry. From this epoch date the bracelets ornamented with little gold plates and engraved turquoises as well as the most diverse figure carvings, which were found in the tomb of Queen Zur, consort of the Pharaoh Athotis. Like malachite, turquoise is a secondary mineral; it developed near the surface from the effect of solvent and percolating meteoric waters, primarily in magmatic rocks in which the ascending underground and the descending rain waters displaced feldspar minerals by their hydrothermal solvent power and dissolved important components from the country rocks; these formed new deposits of turquoise by precipitation from the circulating waters. Chemically speaking, the mineral is a complex hydrous copper-bearing aluminum phosphate, corresponding to the formula $CuAl_6(PO_4)_4(OH)_5 5H_2O$. The strong sky blue can be ascribed to a constituent copper content of less than 10 percent; thus turquoise is ranged within the group of idiochromatic ornamental stones. If traces of iron take the place of copper, the coloring takes on a less admirable greenish tinge. Until recently, when for the first time turquoise became known in obviously triclinic crystal form in the U.S., it was regarded, like opal, as an amorphous stone. After the age-old Sinai mines became largely worked out by the Egyptian slaves, Persia came indisputably into the first rank before the fairly important turquoise-bearing beds of Nevada and Afghanistan. The loveliest light to forget-me-not blue specimens with a fine waxy luster are produced from the famous deposits in the Kuh-i-Binalud mountains, northwest of Nishapur. The older sedimentary rock is here intruded, and in parts even metamorphosed, by younger volcanic rocks consisting of porphyritic trachytes and felsite porphyries, so that turquoise occurs filling cracks and cavities in the brecciated trachyte, and spreading as a closely branching network of narrow veins from 2 to 20 millimeters thick. It was at the same time completely or partly enveloped by the older mineral limonite and intergrown with reticulate patterns, thus producing the turquoise matrix so much prized in the West. The material is not only wrung laboriously from its primary source, but often from weathered masses, talus debris, and water-laid sediments too. New turquoise occurrences have

71 Who would think that unattractive coarse chunks of stone
could shelter such delicate blue and finely veined turquoise?

72 Entrance to the extensive turquoise mines of Abdurrezza near Nishapur in Iran.

recently been traced in northeast Tanzania in the Gilewi Hills. Pliny's observation that *kallait* or *kallalite*—derived from the ancient Greek name *kalos lithos* = "beautiful stone"—could be affected by oils, unguents, and wine is still valid. Turquoise received its present name later, when it entered the European trade via Turkey and the French therefore designated it the *pierre turquoise*, which subsequently became shortened to turquoise. The December stone, turquoise, was eulogized by the oriental poets as talisman of riders and as protector of innocence and good fortune; probably its age-old link with the destinies of mankind may therefore well account for its being veiled in powerful magic. Few gemstones have served to build so harmonious a bridge between the ancients' concept of ornament and the present-day feeling for fashion as turquoise.

73 Turquoise crops out only as narrow veins and restricted cavity fillings in massive trachyte rock, and has to be carefully and laboriously prized from it.

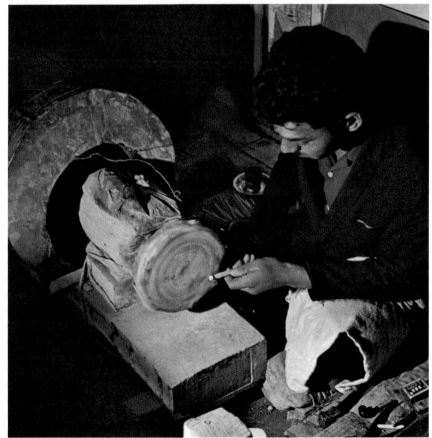

74 In Meshed, a Shiite city of pilgrimage in eastern Iran, turquoises are cut by experienced lapidaries.

Agate Carving and Engraving: The Glyptic Arts

CLEAR crystals make their impact through the magic of color, vividness of luster, and play of light. The enchantment of opaque ornamental stones is kindled by their colors and ravishing color schemes, as well as by the endless array of patterns resulting from their inexhaustible combinations and permutations. Tortuous bands, apparently fortuitously arranged circles, and veinlike swathes of color are the reflection of immutable laws unfathomable in their diversity. Full of continuous surprises and quite unpredictable, they continually pose the cutter new problems, which require from him a high degree of virtuosity. It is not just a case of following the natural circumference of the stone, giving it the prescribed form, and thus fashioning a corresponding object; no less important is the understanding of the course of individual color trends, and—in the unforeseen emergence of a differently colored layering inside the stone—the ability to incorporate it organically and simultaneously into the whole concept of the masterpiece in the process of creation. Inasmuch as he remains the servant of earthborn material, his subtle sensitivity raises the cutter above the status of a mere artisan to a master of his medium. The work of many thousands of years has gone into completing our knowledge of the character of the stone and painstakingly learning its unique rules. Cutting of gemstones seems to have had its origin in India. Even today many of the crystals available in the trade are still cut there. Much later on, Idar-Oberstein, the town on the upper Nahe, took over the leadership in stone cutting, which is still valid today, especially that of colored and ornamental stones, the development of which cannot be separated from its famous agate cutting. Legend has it that the Romans, during the building of their military and trade road from Mainz to Trier, found round stones with pale red and bluish-green banding which resembled the rough stones from the Achates River in Sicily which were cut into ornamental and seal-stones in Imperial Rome. Documentary evidence of lapidaries in Idar-Oberstein dates from 1454, when an indigenous cutting industry began to establish itself there. It made use of the agates from the surrounding hills, principally from the mines of the Steinkaulenberg, where the old tunnels may still be seen. At the beginning of the nineteenth century, when the local occurrences were found to be no longer worth exploiting, unemployment forced many families of cutters to leave home. A few of these migrants, who were wandering through Brazil as itinerant musicians, one day made the remarkable discovery that the

75 Lying in a wooden tub, the agate cutter presses the large piece of agate against the massive sandstone grinding wheel with the whole strength of his body.

courtyard of a homestead was paved with stones showing the unmistakable characteristics of agate. Prospecting resulted in rich finds; their importance for the mother country can be assessed from the fact that since about 1840 Brazil, together with Uruguay, has become the main regular supplier of this raw material. Soon it was accompanied by further treasures from Brazil's rich soil, principally amethyst, aquamarine, topaz, and tourmaline, which, alongside the conventional agate cutting, required a second, refined cutting method—the art of lapidary or colored stone cutting, finally promoting Idar-Oberstein to the status of a metropolis of the gemstone industry, still only surpassed by the diamond-cutting centers of Antwerp and Amsterdam. In the early days of agate cutting the waterpower of the river and its tributaries was used to drive the mighty mill wheels and sandstone grindstones. Lying stomach down across a bench or so-called tipping stool, the cutter held the heavy agate hard against the rotating stone. Although some processes are still carried out according to old custom and with a deal of medieval romanticism, modern technique prevails today, with electric motors and new methods of work. The rough piece is first of all reduced to the approximate size and then cut down on a circular saw impregnated with diamond bort. A wheel charged with carborundum is used for the coarse preparatory grinding, and fine cutting requires sandstone. The final stage is the

76 Smaller pieces of agate receive the rough shape of their final form on the coarse grinding wheel.

77 The cutter of bowls holds the bowl between his knees against the cutting wheel to obtain surer and steadier control.

polishing with tripoli on tin, lead, or felt laps, or on beechwood drums. Cabochons, that is, stones with domed surfaces, are cemented on to a stick for accurate guidance, and cut in narrow grooves on the edges of the grinding wheel.

To unite the fruits of human imagination with beauty is the task of the stone carver or engraver. Glyptics, as the technique of stone carving is called, is one of the oldest branches of art in the Idar-Oberstein agate-cutting industry. It embraces two main spheres. Of these the first is concerned with the production of miniature sculptures and artistic animal models. The astonishing multiplicity of colors and structures, and the varied comeliness of the ornamental stones is thus most wonderfully enhanced by the highly developed artistic sensitivity of the carver. Obvious models, admirably suited for this, are flowers and animals, mainly in graceful forms of tropical birds, whose colored feathers find

127

naturalistic representations in worked stone. A favorite material is pale shimmering rose quartz, one of the massive and rarely macrocrystalline varieties of quartz, colored by manganese. It is worked into bowls, figures, and especially into elephants with uplifted trunks, which in China are regarded as symbols of good luck. The more important part of the glyptic art, however, is the cutting of gems, the zenith of stone carving, which requires from artistically gifted hand workers the most exact knowledge of their material and the greatest precision in their work. The term "gem" is applied in a restricted sense to all gem and ornamental stones carved with pictorial designs. While in cameos the picture is carved in raised relief, intaglios show it in recessed or negative relief. The carving technique remains the same in each case. The derivation of the word "cameo" is probably from the Italian *cammeo,* coming in its turn from the latin *gemma* which gave gemmology its name and which means gemstone. According to other sources it is a loan word from Arabic, in which *chumahän* means agate. By far the most ancient use of engraved gems was in the cylinder seals of Mesopotamia—small hollow rolls of jasper, onyx, sardonyx, or agate, with symbolic or mythological figures and inscriptions cut into them. The impulse which radiated thence in all directions gave rise to an indigenous craft in nearby Egypt. In Mycenaean and Greco-Roman antiquity, pictures with figures developed—signets— whose themes were chosen from myth, the world of gods and nature. With their exceptional feeling for the miniature, the Hellenes raised the art of stone carving to superlative heights. The Byzantine and, in part, also the Romanesque eras produced a number of large cameos, which were used as decorative pieces in crosses, reliquary shrines, and altar tables. The withering of the early Greek culture then interrupted the blossoming of the glyptic art for hundreds of years. It flickered into short-lived existence in the late antique period during the reign of Constantine in the fourth century and in the twelfth century at the court of Frederick in Sicily, to culminate in a renewed zenith during the Quattrocento, in the periods of the Renaissance and of classicism. Some of the most sublime pictorial works were created in the course of these epochs. One of the most exquisite is the Tazza Farnese, a shallow bowl of white and brown sardonyx; it once belonged to Lorenzo the Magnificent, and may be seen in the National Museum of Naples. As barter for one of the most famous cameos, the *Gemma Augustea* (Augustan Gem), which is ascribed to the hand of the great Dioscorides, Pope Paul II made an offer to the town of Toulouse, in whose walls it was then to be found, to build a bridge over the Garonne, but in vain. Considered second only to the latter, the still larger sardonyx cameo *Le Grand Camée de France* (the Great Cameo of France), now exhibited in the Cabinet des Médailles of the Paris National Library, is said to have been made by one of Dioscorides' sons—Herophilos, Eutyches, or Hyllos. In 1961 the Würtemberg Provincial Museum in Stuttgart was able to acquire the well-known Jupiter Cameo of Gotha, a splendid multilayered sardonyx. Onyx and sardonyx are the preferred members of the quartz group for carving cameos and intaglios. The varicolored layers of these minerals most easily

79 Gemstone flower spray. The "bleeding hearts" are carved from rhodochrosite and the green leaves from serpentine; the stem is of beaten gold and the little vase formed of rock crystal.

allow the sculpturing of a polychromatic design. Usually the images are raised in light color from a dark brown or bluish-black background after the manner of a silhouette, the optical effect of strongly contrasting colors being consciously sought, because of the small size. It would be difficult to pick out names of the highest rank in the list of numerous masters of the glyptic art, all the more since we mostly depend on conjecture; moreover, many stone carvers of later times signed their gems with Greek names. Dioscorides, a contemporary of Pliny, his sons, and the stone carvers Epitynchanos and Skylax must be mentioned, likewise Natter and Pichler who, in the age of Winckelmann (eighteenth century) turned once again to the relicts of antiquity, and, in the present, the works of Martin Seitz and Richard Hahn, so highly prized by art connoisseurs. Their creations, all of which are pictorial, are made from the most noble minerals which have been entrusted to man from the darkness of the earth. He already made use, as early as the preliterary Sumerian epoch, of the rotating drill to breathe life into the precious material; today, he needs technology and the diamond-impregnated steel point with which to amalgamate the images of his fancy with the valuable stone into an artistic unity.

129

Appreciation of Gemstones

IN this epilogue the author would like to express the hope that he has furnished an explanatory and stimulating account to his readers, both feminine and masculine, by leading them into many an unfamiliar corner of an extensive and mystery-shrouded kingdom. Certainly, it would be interesting for laymen, who probably in their earliest childhood first made acquaintance in fairytales with the magic world of gemstones, to study the role of these self-same stones in the folklore of countries, peoples, and times. However, in this book it was intentional to keep the rational and purely scientific side of gemstones as seen from a gemmologist's viewpoint in the foreground, so that, for once, fact-hungry laymen might be given comprehensible answers to such burning questions as, "What is a gemstone?"; "Why is it so valuable?"; "What causes its beautiful colors?"; "Where and how was it actually formed and how is it found today?" In contrast to most books on gemstones this one was also designed from the outset to describe more fully by means of both text and illustrations the evolution and mining of the most beautiful minerals. It is precisely the long history of development—from the enormous forces of the earth, through the indescribable toil and sweat involved in their recovery, to the sensitive completion on the cutting lap—which has wrought a gemstone into a most costly gift of Nature; it is one which induces in the wearer so much marvelling awe of the glittering gemstone, which in fulfillment of its destiny is at last mounted as an enchanting jewel. On exactly this ground, too, it is false and misleading to call artificial or synthetic stones gemstones, for those are products manufactured in laboratories by the hand of man, completely without rarity or natural origin. Moreover, that ghastly term "semiprecious stone" is a linguistic monstrosity which should be avoided, because it results in considerable harm to the popularity of the stone so described. Today a distinction is made between "gemstones" and "ornamental stones," whereby in general the former is applied to transparent gems and the latter to the opaque ones.

> Like flowers, we saw gemstones
> Sparkling in the brilliance of light;
>
> Brought forth by Nature as crystals,
> Chosen by man as jewels.

80 A quetzal made from various ornamental stones invisibly joined—a true
masterpiece of the stone carver's art—on a mineral base of apophyllite.

Glossary of Technical Terms

Abbreviations used in the description of minerals:

S.G. = specific gravity
H   = hardness
R.I. = refractive index

Adamantine: designation for the particularly high luster of diamond (derived from the Greek *adamas* = diamond).

Adularescence: the phenomenon of the bluish-white, wavering shimmer of light on moonstone (q.v.) caused by interference of light on the alternating lamellae of soda- and potash-feldspars (q.v.)

Agate: variety of chalcedony (q.v.) with banded structure in differently colored layers. SiO_2 (silica). S.G. = 2.6; H = 7; R.I. = 1.53.

Alexandrite: a variety of chrysoberyl (q.v.) which changes from green (in daylight) to red (in artificial light). $BeAl_2O_4$. S.G. = 3.71; H = 8.5; R.I. = 1.75.

Allochromatic- means "foreign-colored"; refers to minerals whose coloring is caused by extraneous admixtures (which are not constituent parts of the chemical composition).

Alluvium: a general term for all detrital deposits resulting from recent operations of rivers, thus including the sediments deposited in river beds, flood plains, lakes, talus hills, and fans at the foot of slopes and estuaries. Also called gem placers.

Almandine: the iron-bearing variety of garnet (q.v.), thus an iron-alumina garnet. $Fe_3Al_2(SiO)_4)_3$. Brownish-red to violet. S.G. = 3.9–4.2; H = 7.5; R.I. = 1.76–1.81.

Amblygonite: uncommon gemstone (collectors' stone). Chemically a lithium-aluminium-phosphate $(LiAl[OH, F]PO_4)$. Colorless to golden yellow. S.G. = 3.0; H = 6; R.I. = 1.610–1.636.

Amethyst: light to dark violet variety of macrocrystalline quartz. SiO_2. S.G. = 2.65; H = 7; R.I. = 1.548.

Amethyst-almond: almond-shaped druse (q.v.) whose inner surface is encrusted with amethyst.

Amorphous: literally "shapeless"; refers to minerals with no definite crystalline structure (no regular arrangement of their atoms) and consequently displaying no definite external shape. They are noncrystalline minerals in contradistinction to crystals.

Andalusite: unusual gemstone (collectors' stone) of green and red-brown color. Al_2SiO_5. Strongly pleochroic (q.v.). S.G. = 3.15; H = 7.5; R.I. = 1.64.

Apatite: uncommon gemstone (collectors' stone) which occurs in almost all colors. Complex chemical composition: $Ca_5(PO_4)_3(F, Cl, OH)$. S.G. = 3.21; H = 5; R.I. = 1.638.

Apophyllite: normally colorless, but also reddish, greenish, or bluish, strikingly platy sheetlike mineral (apo = away, up; phyllon = leaf). Treasured by collectors as an ornamental stone. S.G. = 2.3–2.5; H = 4.5–5; R.I. = 1.535–1.545.

Aquamarine: light blue to greenish-blue colored variety of beryl (q.v.). $Be_3Al_2Si_6O_{18}$. S.G. = 2.69; H = 7.5; R.I. = 1.575.

Asterism: the optical phenomenon of starlike lines of light on cabochon-cut gemstones, caused by reflection of the incident light on suitably oriented inclusions (q.v.).

Azurite: radial aggregates of azure-blue color. $Cu_3(CO_3)_2(OH)_2$. Related to malachite (q.v.). S.G. = 3.8; H = 3.5–4; R.I. = 1.73–1.86.

Baguette: narrow rectangular rod-shaped cut style of gemstones (chiefly for diamond).

Benitoite: very rare gemstone (collectors' stone) of sapphire-blue color. $BaO TiO_2, SiO_2$. S.G. = 3.67; H = 6.5; R.I. = 1.78.

Beryl: important group of vari-colored gemstones of typical pegmatitic origin (q.v.). Varieties: aquamarine, emerald, golden beryl, goshenite, heliodor, morganite, and many others. $Be_3Al_2(Si_6O_{18})$. S.G. = 2.68–2.80; H = 7.5; R.I. = 1.57.1.59.

Brazilianite: unusual gemstone (collectors' stone) of yellowish-green to greenish-yellow color. $NaAl_3(OH)_4(PO_4)_2$. S.G. = 2.99; H = 5.5; R.I. = 1.612.

Breccia: sedimentary rock (q.v.) composed mostly of sharp and angular rock fragments (detrital material) cemented together.

Brilliance: the term comprises all optical properties which affect light falling on a cut gemstone.

Cameo- from the Italian *cameo*: carved ornamental stone (= gem, q.v.) with raised pictorial design.

Carat: the unit of weight for all gemstones and for cultured pearls. One carat is one-fifth of a gram (= 0.20 gm.).

Carnelian: reddish-brown, brown, or brownish-red chalcedony (q.v.) which, in ancient times, was used primarily for carving gems (q.v.).

Cat's-eyes: cabochon-cut ornamental stones over whose convex surface a bright line of light wanders when the stone is turned. This unusual phenomenon appears in various gemstones, especially chrysoberyl, but also in quartz, tourmaline, aquamarine, and many others.

Cesium: chemical element; symbol Cs; rare alkali metal; trace element in rose-red beryl (morganite).

Chalcedony group: compact massive cryptocrystalline, that is, microscopically fine crystalline quartz in various colors and color intensities. Translucent to opaque. SiO_2. S.G. = 2.6; H = 7; R.I. = 1.53.

Chatoyancy: derived from the French *chat* = cat. Means the occurrence of a wavering shimmer of light, which moves over the domed or hemispherical surface of a gemstone as a narrow line of light reminiscent of the slit pupil of a cat's eye. The phenomenon arises from reflection of incident light by fine parallel fibers in the interior of the gemstone.

Chemogenous- chemically produced. Colors determined by the chemistry of the gemstone.

Chromogenous: forming of coloring matter; in transferred sense: color-imparting.

Chromophorous: bearing coloring matter; in transferred sense: colored.

Chrysoberyl: important and valuable gemstone, distinguished by forming three completely different varieties: alexandrite, chrysoberyl, and cat's-eye (also called cymophane). $BeAl_2O_4$. S.G. = 3.71; H = 8.5; R.I. = 1.75.

Chrysolite: old name, no longer acceptable, for peridot (q.v.), a variety of olivine.

Chrysoprase: fine green chalcedony (q.v.) colored by nickel. SiO_2. S.G. = 2.6; H = 7; R.I. = 1.52.

Citrine: yellow- to brown-colored variety of crystalline quartz and also the yellow, brown to red-brown variety produced by heating amethyst, which is often falsely and erroneously called in the trade topaz. S.G. = 2.65; H = 7; R.I. = 1.548.

Cobalt- chemical element, symbol Co: steel-gray glittering magnetic metal often used as a coloring agent to product a blue color in synthetic stones and glasses.

Cohesion: the internal force of attraction (bond strength) of the molecules of a body.

Colloidal: matter in the finest distribution dissolved in another material, e.g., solid in liquid = colloidal solution.

Colored stones: see Fancy stones.

Conglomerate: a clastic sedimentary rock, whose rounded waterworn component fragments (detrital rocks) are cemented together.

Constituent- related to the construction: determined by its situation; belonging to the atoms of a molecule.

Contact metamorphism: every alteration of rock caused by contact with uprising molten rock masses (magma).

Contact minerals: minerals which have resulted from the process of contact metamorphism (q.v.).

Contact rock: rock which has either been involved in the process of contact metamorphism or has originated from a contact metamorphism.

Cordierite: uncommon gemstone (collectors' stone) with strong pleochroism (q.v.) (blue, pale brown, gray-blue). Also called iolite or dichroite. $Mg_2Al_4Si_5O_{18}$. S.G. = 2.6; H = 7; R.I. = 1.535.

Corundum: name of the minerals (gemstones) which consist of crystalline alumina (aluminium oxide = Al_2O_3). Famous varieties are red ruby and blue sapphire. S.G. = 3.99; H = 9; R.I. = 1.765.

Crown facets: the sloping facets which form the crown (part above the girdle) of the brilliant cut (but also of other cuts, such as marquise, navette, pear-shape, etc.).

Cryptocrystalline: describes mineral aggregates which consist of submicroscopically fine crystals so that the individual components cannot be seen with a magnifying lens; in contrast to aggregates whose mineral components are macroscopic, i.e., can be recognized with the unaided eye.

Cubic: also called regular or isometric; the descriptive term for those crystal classes which are characterized by an axial intersection with three equal axes at right angles to one another.

Cullet: the name of the small facet which frequently truncates the point of the pavilion of the brilliant cut (or other cuts, such as navette, marquise, baguette, pear-shape).

Cymophane: another name for chrysoberyl cat's-eye.

Dagoba (Ceylonese): Buddhist reliquary shrine (pagoda).

Danburite: rare gemstone (collectors' stone); light to wine yellow from Burma, colorless from Japan, and rose-red from Mexico. S.G. = 3; H = 7; R.I. = 1.633.

Demantoid: very brilliant variety of andradite garnet with vivid yellowish green color. Very rare. $Ca_3Fe_2(SiO_4)_3$. Colored by chromium. S.G. = 3.85; H = 6.5; R.I. = 1.89.

Dendritic- derived from the Greek *dendron* = tree: the word means tree-shaped or fernlike ramifying patterns of iron or manganese oxides in minerals or on bedding planes.

Derivative = something derived from (something else): results of a geochemical process, e.g., the Jurassic limestone, which is produced by sedimentation.

Desilication: the removal of silica from a rock as it occurs in the metamorphism (alteration) of rocks.

Diamond: chemically pure carbon, crystallizing in the cubic system, C. Occurs colorless and in all colors. It is distinguished by its great hardness and high refractive index. One of the most valuable precious stones and a most important material in industry and technology. S.G. = 3.52; H = 10; R.I. = 2.4175.

Diorite: granular, mostly greenish-black plutonic rock, which in the gradation from acid rocks (granite) to basic rocks (gabbro) falls approximately in the middle.

Dispersed form: scattered or finely divided form.

Dop: tool to which a gemstone is cemented or firmly fastened during the cutting process and on which it is mounted when brought on to the cutting lap.

Druse (crystal druse): a cavity in the rock lined with crystals (e.g., rock crystal, amethyst, calcite, etc.) but with a remaining central space.

Dullam (Ceylonese): residue of heavy minerals in the wash basket.

Eclogite: a granular rock composed essentially of garnet (almandine-pyrope) and pyroxene.

Eluvial: name given to rotten rocks and weathered soils which have developed immediately above the still coherent bedrock.

Emerald: green variety of beryl, colored by chromium. Gemstone quality very rare. $Be_3Al_2Si_6O_{18}$. S.G. = 2.71; H = 7.5; R.I. = 1.575.

Emerald-cut: so-called trap cut or rectangular form with truncated corners, used mainly for emeralds but also for diamonds (emerald cut), and popular for aquamarine, morganite, topaz, tourmaline, and many other gemstones.

Enstatite: unusual gemstone (collectors' stone) of the pyroxene mineral group, of green, brownish-green, or brown color. $Mg_2Si_2O_6$. S.G. = 3.27; H = 5.5; R.I. = 1.67.

Essonite: yellow brown to brownish red variety of the calcium aluminium garnet grossular (q.v.). It is occasionally called cinnamon stone. $Ca_3Al_2(SiO_4)_3$. S.G. = 3.65; H = 7.25; R.I. = 1.74.

Euclase: very rare gemstone (collectors' stone) colorless or of light green or light blue color, primarily from Brazil. Be (AlOH) SiO_4. S.G. = 3.10; H = 7.5; R.I. = 1.665.

Exsolution: unmixing of the components of a mixed crystal.

Falcon's-eye: cryptocrystalline (q.v.) quartz with fine fibrous inclusions of the blue mineral crocidolite (a variety of asbestos). It is blue because it has not undergone oxidation and is characterized by a cat's-eye effect (chatoyancy, q.v.). Closely related to tiger's-eye (q.v.).

Fancy (color) stones: term often used, but not an official classification, of gemstones which are prized for their characteristic colors e.g., ruby, sapphire, emerald, aquamarine, garnet, peridot, topaz, tourmaline, zircon, among many others. With diamond the term refers to the color varieties (e.g. fancy diamond).

Fayalite: iron-rich, magnesium-poor end member of the isomorphous series of olivines (*see* peridot). Fe_2SiO_4.

Feldspar: by far the most important group of rock-forming minerals, with many varieties. The following feldspars are valued as gem or ornamental stones: albite, amazonite, aventurine, labradorite, microcline, moonstone, orthoclase, sunstone (oligoclase), and spectrolite. Their properties vary according to their chemical composition.

Fire opal: rare transparent, mostly rather hazy opal of an orange color. Rarely with play of color. From Mexico. $SiO_2 + nH_2O$. S.G. = 2.00; H = 6; R.I. = 1.45.

Fluorite: uncommon gemstone, also called fluorspar, which occurs in all colors, mostly in light shades. CaF_2. S.G. = 3.18; H = 4; R.I. = 1.434.

Forsterite: the iron-poor, magnesium-rich end member of the isomorphous series of olivines (*see* peridot). Mg_2SiO_4.

Gabbro: magnesium-rich, silica-poor, and thus basic plutonic rock, of blackish-green color and granular texture.

Garnet: large group of isomorphous crystals with many varicolored varieties which are determined by differences in their chemical composition. The following gemstone varieties are identified by their chemical makeup and resulting color: almandine, andradite, demantoid, grossular, essonite, melanite, pyrope, rhodolite, spessartite, and uvarovite.

Gem: (a) a general term for any precious stone, such as diamond, ruby, sapphire, emerald, but also spinel, topaz, tourmaline, etc.; (b) carved ornamental stone with raised (cameo) or recessed (intaglio, used as a seal) pictorial design. Derived from the Latin word *gemma* for gemstone.

Gem gravel: minable concentration of usable minerals or gemstones in surface deposits (gravel, sand, valley detritus, river debris, etc.) which have been laid down in the geological present by the action of water (rain, river transport).

Gemmologist: the word is derived from the Latin word *gemma* = gemstone, and means a person who is concerned with the science of gemstones (= gemmology).

Gemmology = gem knowledge: science of gemstones, derived from the Latin *gemma* = gemstone and the Greek *logos* = learning/teaching/science.

Glyptic: the art of working, with chisel and scorper, in stone or metal—the art of stone carving. (Gemnoglyptic = the art of carving gems (q.v.).)

Gneiss: widely distributed, metamorphic rock in the crystalline schist group. Main components are as in granite: quartz, feldspar, and mica. Texture is mostly foliated.

Grossular: Calcium aluminium garnet $Ca_3Al_2(SiO_4)_3$, a calcium-bearing variety of the garnet group, of green and yellow to brownish-red color, transparent to opaque. S.G. = 3.65; H = 7.25; R.I. = 1.74.

Harlequin opal: opal whose dazzling color flecks exhibit geometrical forms and are of equal size, rather like a chessboard or just like a harlequin's suit.

Haüynite: predominantly deep blue mineral of cubic symmetry. It is a sodium aluminium silicate and a component of lapis lazuli (q.v.).

Hexagonal = six-sided: the collective name of those crystal classes which are characterized by an axial intersection with one sixfold main axis and three equal horizontal axes intersecting in one plane at 120°, e.g. beryl.

Hiddenite: named after its discoverer (W. E. Hidden), the shining green variety, colored by chromium, of the spodumene gemstone group; the other color varieties bear the family name except for the lilac kunzite (discovered by the New York gemmologist F. Kunz). $LiAlSi_2O_6$. S.G. = 3.18; H = 7; R.I. = 1.67.

Hydrothermal phase: the last stage of the deposits and their minerals directly formed from magmas, which in this phase emanated from hot watery solutions.

Idiochromatic: = self-colored, i.e. gem and ornamental stones, in which the coloring pigment is a constituent part of the chemical composition.

Illam (Ceylonese): the gemmiferous gravel of the alluvial deposits in the island of Ceylon.

Imperial Jade: designation of the finest emerald-green colored jadeite, tinted by chromium.

Inclusions: foreign matter (solid, fluid or gaseous) in gemstones, which was trapped during the host crystal's growth, or crystallized out of enclosed supersaturated solutions, or resulted from mechanical pressure, tension, or structural alteration. They affect the clarity and thereby the transparency of gemstones, but on the other hand serve as important evidence of genuineness and of source.

Interference of light: the phenomenon of mutual influence and superposition of two homogeneous light waves of similar frequency and closely adjoining direction of propagation, whereby they produce a shift of light, whose position and nature results from the individual components.

Iolite: See cordierite.

Ion (plural: ions): electrically positively or negatively charged atoms (atomic ion) or molecules (molecular ion).

Isomorphs: minerals in which certain atoms can be replaced by others of similar chemical nature (e.g. Mn for Fe = spessartite-almandine) or the stoicheiometric ratio of the constituents may be altered (e.g. 80 percent Mg + 20 percent Fe = pyrope or 30 percent Mg + 70 percent Fe = almandine) without changing the crystal structure and form.

Jade: collective name for the two similar-looking but chemically and structurally different minerals, jadeite and nephrite (q.v.).

Jadeite: an opaque variety of spodumene, one of the minerals belonging to the large group of the pyroxenes, and included among the ornamental stones; at the same time one of the two minerals going under the collective name of jade. Mostly massive (microcrystalline fibers matted together), it occurs in green, white, yellow, brown, pink, and violet shades, according to the pigmenting agent. $NaAlSi_2O_6$. S.G. = 3.33; H = 7; R.I. = 1.66.

Jade minerals: under this designation, strictly only the two ornamental stones jadeite and nephrite (q.v.) are understood. In a wider sense, however, the concept includes other jadelike minerals, such as chloromelanite and jade-albite.

Jasper: old miners' name: collective term for compact (crystalline) nontransparent quartz of varying colorings (often incorrectly applied to the dark green, red-spotted, cryptocrystalline quartz, heliotrope/bloodstone).

Jasperized serpentine: silicified serpentine rock. Serpentine (q.v.) which has become intensively intergrown by silica or even converted into silica, by means of impregnating siliceous waters.

Kimberlite: brecciated diamond-bearing serpentinelike blue-green variety of mica peridotite ("blue ground"), one of the basic plutonic rocks mainly consisting of olivine and phlogopite. Kimberlite forms the "fill" of the primary deposits of diamonds, known as "pipe mines" (volcanic necks).

Labradorescence: the colored iridescence of labradorite and spectrolite.

Labradorite: blue and green shimmering ornamental stone of the large feldspar family (q.v.). The variety with multicolored shimmer, from Finland, is also called spectrolite. S.G. = 2.7; H = 6–6.5; R.I. = 1.565. In its noblest form labradorite occurs as a transparent yellow gemstone.

Lapis lazuli: a rock, i.e., a mixture of various minerals, of which the most important are lazurite, diopside, and calcite. It is dark blue, frequently traversed by whitish flecks of calcite, and recognizable by the many minute inclusions of golden, shining pyrite. S.G. = 2.8; H = 5.5; R.I. = 1.5.

Leucosapphire: fancy name for colorless sapphire (not used very much today).

Limonite: aqueous iron oxide which forms so-called concretions. It is often the mother rock (matrix) (q.v.) of turquoise, simultaneously penetrating it with branching veins.

Liquid-magmatic: liquid-magmatic formations are rocks (e.g. granite) and deposits (such as labradorite, peridot, and zircon) which have evolved from the viscous components of the magma.

Lithosphere: the term is derived from the Greek *lithos* = stone, and means the shell of our earth (earth's crust), made up of rocks.

Macroscopic: visible to the unaided eye (in contrast to microscopic).

Magma: liquid silicate melt (nonvolatile components) saturated with gases (volatile components) enclosed within the earth's interior, which may extrude at the earth's surface by means of volcanic eruptions.

Magmatic: consisting of magma (q.v.). A magmatic succession is the formation of all rocks and minerals which have crystallized from the molten parts of the deeper crust of the earth, that is, from the magma.

Magmatic cycle: the process by which all types of igneous rocks and their minerals have formed from the molten parts of the deeper earth's crust, i.e., likewise the magma.

Malachite: a predominantly close-fibered weathering product of copper deposits, forming botryoidal aggregates. Green, usually banded like agate. $CuCO_3Cu (OH)_2$. S.G. = 3.8; H = 4; R.I. = 1.78.

Manganese: chemical element, symbol Mn; silvery gray, hard, very brittle metal; constituent component of several gem and ornamental stones (rhodochrosite, rhodonite, spessartite).

Manganese minerals: minerals which contain appreciable contents of manganese and are thus often idiochromatically (q.v.) colored,

e.g. rhodochrosite, rhodonite, psilomelanite, pyrolusite, (q.v.) and many others.

Marble: metamorphic (i.e. subsequently altered) granular limestone (in the technical sense, any limestone or dolomite capable of taking a polish).

Marquise: long, ship-shaped cut form, mostly used for diamonds.

Matrix: the natural rock in which minerals occur interbedded (= mother rock).

Melaphyre rocks: dark, often dense, but also porous, eruptive rocks of differing composition, e.g. basalt. Also called extrusive rocks.

Metamorphic = altered, from "metamorphism" = alteration. The alteration of mineral parageneses after their deposition, by external action such as contact with magmatic rocks, regional changes in the pressure and temperature (e.g. contact metamorphic limestone, crystalline schists, etc.).

Metamorphic cycle: process by which consolidated rocks are altered in composition, texture, or internal structure through pressure, heat and new chemical substances.

Methylene iodide test = an application of the so-called suspension method. The principle is based on the fact that substances of higher specific gravity sink in a given liquid, while those of lower specific gravity float, e.g. stone and wood respectively in water. To determine the specific gravity of gem and ornamental stones, gemmologists often use the so-called heavy liquids. One of these is methylene iodide, with a density of 3.33. High gravity gemstones, e.g. topaz (S.G. = 3.53–3.56) sink in it, while lighter gemstones, e.g. citrine (S.G. = 2.65), float.

Mica: group of important rock-building minerals of mostly sheetlike laminated structure. Best known are the colorless shining silvery muscovite, the brown viotite, and the green fuchsite. Chemically the micas are complex aluminium silicates.

Mica schists: general term for a group of metamorphic rocks in the crystalline schist class characterized by a high content of quartzose and micaceous minerals and a low one of feldspar.

Monoclinic = singly inclined. The monoclinic crystal system comprises all those crystal classes which are characterized by an axial intersection of three axes of unequal length, of which two (a and c) intersect at an acute angle, while the third (b) is at right-angles to both.

Moonstone: colorless, whitish, green, brown to black translucent feldspar (orthoclase) with a shimmering light effect (*see* adularescence). S.G. = 2.57; H = 6; R.I. = 1.53.

Morion (smoky quartz): dark smoke-brown to almost black smoky quartz. S.G. = 2.65; H = 7; R.I. = 1.548.

Mother rock: term for the rock in which gem and ornamental stones have been formed contemporaneously or after its cooling.

Navette: longish, pointed oval, ship-shaped form of cut (see also marquise), used mainly for diamond.

Nephrite: a hornblende mineral of the amphibole group with complex chemical composition. It is one of the two ornamental stones included under the general term jade. It forms extremely dense, microscopically fibrous, matted aggregates of dark green, brown, yellow, gray, and white hues. S.G. = 2.96; H = 6.5; R.I. = 1.62.

Octahedron: crystal form of the cubic crystal system, bounded by eight equilateral triangles, i.e. two four-sided pyramids with their basal planes back to back.

Olivine: group of vitreous, yellowish to olive- and bottle-green translucent to transparent silicate minerals, whose iron/magnesium content occurs in varying ratios $(Mg, Fe)_2SiO_4$. Important constituent of the basic peridotite rocks and of kimberlite (q.v.). The gem variety peridot occurs in the center of the Mg-Fe isomorphous series, between the end members of fayalite and forsterite (q.v.).

Onyx: agate (q.v.) with alternating white and black layers (mostly artificially colored). S.G. = 2.65; H = 7; R.I. = 1.53.

Opal: amorphous, hydrated silica $SiO_2.nH_2O$. Colorless, white, black, orange, and varicolored. As a result of interference and diffraction of incident light it exhibits a flashing play of spectrum colors. S.G. = 2.0–2.1; H = 6; R.I. = 1.45.

Ornamental stones: in the wider sense, all minerals suitable for jewelry and ornamental purposes; in the narrow sense, all opaque, nontransparent minerals, such as agate, jade, lapis lazuli, malachite, rhodochrosite, rhodonite, turquoise, etc.

Orthoclase: member of the feldspar group (potash feldspar $KAlSi_3O_8$). In gem quality, clear, transparent and golden yellow. Main component of moonstone (q.v.). S.G. = 2.67; H = 6; R.I. = 1.53.

Paragenesis: The association of minerals as a result of their related evolution side by side or one after the other.

Pavilion facets: facets below the girdle of a cut gemstone, which comprises an upper part (crown) and a lower part (pavilion).

Pegmatite: liquid–magmatic or pneumatolytic rocks which have developed as intrusives out of residual granitic melts and generally form very coarse-grained veins or lenses in granitic or syenitic rocks (q.v.). Pegmatites are characterized by minerals of the rare and volatile elements, especially lithium, cesium, boron, beryllium, etc., but also by rare earths like thorium, uranium, and others. Many gemstones, such as beryl, topaz, tourmaline, and others, are found in pegmatites. Main components of pegmatites are quartz and feldspar.

Pegmatite mineral: mineral which has developed from a pegmatitic rock or mineral formation.

Pegmatitic: derived from pegmatite formation and in pegmatite veins or their immediate neighborhood.

Pegmatitic phase: one of the very important stages, for gemstone formation, of the magmatic cycle of ore deposits and mineral formation (*see* pegmatite).

Peridot: olive green, spinach- or pistachio-green olivine (q.v.) of gemstone quality. Thanks to its chemical composition it occurs exactly in the middle of the olivine group between the end members, fayalite and forsterite, in that it contains iron and magnesium in equal amounts. $(Fe,Mg)_2SiO_4$. S.G. = 3.34; H = 6.5; R.I. = 1.67.

Phenakite: uncommon gemstone (collectors' stone), always colorless. Chemically a beryllium silicate: Be_2SiO_4. S.G. = 2.96; H = 7.5; R.I. = 1.662.

Phenomenal stones: gemstones which are distinguished by some unusual effect of light (= phenomenon), e.g. adularescence, asterism, chatoyancy (q.v.).

Pleochroism: the property of anisotropic (that is, doubly refractive) crystals, which, because of the dissimilar or selective absorption of light, show different colors in different directions, e.g. alexandrite, iolite, kunzite, tourmaline, and many others.

Pneumatolytic: mineral formations in which mainly the superheated volatile components liberated from the congealing magma have been involved. A number of gemstones owe their origin to pneumatolysis, e.g., emerald, topaz, tourmaline.

Pneumatolytic deposits: those which have resulted from pneumatolytic mineral formation.

Prase opal: fancy name for green opal colored by included nickel. $SiO_2 + nH_2O$. S.G. = 2.1; H = 6; R.I. = 1.45.

Praseolite: green variety of quartz, whose color is achieved by heating certain amethyst and yellowish quartz from a source at Montezuma, Rio Pardo district, Minas Gerais, Brazil. S.G. = 2.65; H = 7; R.I. = 1.548.

Prism: columnar crystal form whose faces intersect two axes of the axial cross and are parallel to the third (vertical) axis. In optics, a five-sided wedge-shaped body cut from glass.

Pseudomorph: mineral in the crystal form proper to another mineral, which it has replaced by substitution or by chemical alteration.

Pseudomorphism: process of replacement of one mineral by another.

Pyrope: fiery- to blood-red magnesium-rich variety of garnet (q.v.), thus a magnesium aluminium garnet. $Mg_3Al_2(SiO_4)_3$. S.G. = 3.7–3.9; H = 72.5; R.I. = 1.73–1.76.

Quartz: crystallized pure silica (SiO_2), widespread rock-forming mineral; in gem quality, originating in the pegmatitic and hydrothermal phases.

Gem varieties: amethyst, citrine, praseolite, rock crystal, rose quartz, smoky quartz.

Finely crystalline and cryptocrystalline (q.v.) ornamental stones: agate, chalcedony, chrysoprase, jasper, among many others. S.G. = 2.6–2.65; H = 7; R.I. = 1.53–1.548.

Quetzal: fruit-eating tropical bird with long tail feathers, found in the rain forests of southern Mexico and down as far as Panama. Name is of Aztec origin.

Rhodochrosite: rose-red marbled or banded ornamental stone, also called manganese spar. $MnCo_3$. A prized decorative stone, originating as stalagmites. S.G. = 3.6; H = 4; R.I. = 1.71.

Rhodonite: ornamental stone of rose-red to dark-red color, often traversed by black spots and patterns. $CaMn_4[Si_5O_{15}]$ = manganese silicate. S.G. = 3.65; H = 6; R.I. = 1.73.

Rhombododecahedron: a growth form bounded by twelve congruent rhombs. Frequent habit of crystals crystallizing in the cubic system, e.g. diamond, garnet, etc.

*Rhombic (*also called *orthorhombic):* all those crystals whose faces are referred to an axial intersection of three unequal axes all at right angles to each other. They have a rectangular or rhomb-shaped basal plane.

Rose quartz: pink-colored, mostly milky or cloudy quartz colored by manganese, which seldom develops individual crystals but usually occurs as finely crystalline compact masses. Favorite jewelry and ornamental stone. SiO_2. S.G. = 2.65; H = 7; R.I. = 1.548.

Rough stones: rough, that is, uncut minerals or gemstones.

Ruby: red variety of corundum (q.v.) colored red by a small chromium content. Al_2O_3. S.G. = 3.99; H = 9; R.I. = 1.765.

Rutile (rutile needles): dark reddish-brown to black mineral of titanium oxide, crystallizing in the tetragonal system. Often forms inclusions (q.v.) in andalusite, garnet, corundum, and quartz, and, when at its most delicate as minute needles, is responsible for asterism (q.v.). S.G. = 4.25; H = 6; R.I. = 2.62 –2.90.

Sapphire: variety, colored blue by titanium, of corundum (q.v.), and thus a brother mineral of ruby. Al_2O_3. The term "sapphire" is often used for colorless, yellow, green, pink, violet, and black varieties, which owe their hues partly to different valencies of the iron as a coloring agent. S.G. = 3.99; H = 9; R.I. = 1.765.

Sard: brown to reddish chalcedony (q.v.). The related sardonyx is a red and white banded chalcedony, very popular for carving engraved gems. S.G. = 2.6; H = 7; R.I. = 1.53.

Scapolite: unusual gemstone (collectors' stone) of yellow, pink, and blue shades, but also colorless. Vitreous luster, transparent. The pink variety often occurs as cat's-eyes (q.v.). Complex silicate. S.G. = 2.63–2.70; H = 6; R.I. = 1.545–1.57.

Scheelite: calcium wolframite ($CaWO_4$); very rare gemstone of yellowish-white, golden yellow, or brown to orange-yellow color, with adamantine luster. S.G. = 6; H = 4.5; R.I. = 1.925.

Secondary detritus: secondary deposits (so-called gem gravels (q.v.). Mineral parageneses which have been transported from their sources and are now to be found at a second site of deposition, e.g. river detritus, stream sediments, valley-bottom silts, etc.

Sedimentary = resulting from sedimentation, that is, deposition from water. The sedimentary processes include all means whereby rocks and minerals are broken down and redeposited through reworking or new formation of rocks and minerals on the earth's surface, in waters, and in the uppermost crust of the earth.

Sedimentary rocks: the layered and detrital rocks formed by the accumulation of sediment in water (e.g. dolomite, limestone, conglomerate, sandstone, shale, etc.).

Sedimentation: the formation and consolidation of detrital and layered rocks by the forces of transportation, such as wind, water, and ice, and by precipitation out of springs, rivers, lakes, and seas.

Selective absorption: differential, i.e. unequal, absorption of light as it travels through a substance.

Serpentine: A common rock-forming mineral; serpentine rocks are weathering products, which have developed mainly through alteration of olivine rocks (q.v.). They furnish popular ornamental stones. Serpentine minerals, e.g. bonamite, also serve as jewelry stones, especially because of their similarity to jade (q.v.). $Mg_6(OH)_8Si_4O_{10}$. S.G. = 2.5–2.6; H = 2–4; R.I. = 1.56.

Shelf banks: sand banks in the shallow-water zone of the sea down to 200 meters depth of water. The continental shelf is considered as part of the continent, surrounding it with a narrow or broad fringe.

Sial: uppermost zone of the earth's crust (lithosphere), in whose composition the main components are silica and alumina.

Silicates: combinations of silica (generally silicon dioxide SiO_2) with bases, of which the most common are potassium, sodium, calcium, magnesium, iron, and aluminium.

Sima: the lower zone of the earth's crust, principally composed of silica and magnesia, from which the mainly basic rocks have evolved.

Sinhalite (from Sinhala, Sanskrit name for Ceylon): uncommon gemstone of yellowish to deep brown color, transparent, with vitreous luster. $Mg(Al,Fe)BO_4$. S.G. = 3.48; H = 6.5; R.I. = 1.685.

Smoky quartz: smoke-brown variety of quartz (q.v.), colored by the effect of cosmic rays. SiO_2. S.G. = 2.65; H = 7; R.I. = 1.548.

Sodalite: opaque, mainly dark blue, but also greenish, yellowish, or gray mineral with complex chemical composition. Important color-imparting component of lapis lazuli (q.v.). Occurs abundantly in Canada, where sodalite is used as a jewelry and ornamental stone.

Spectrolite: the variety of labradorite (q.v.) which shimmers in all the colors of the rainbow (= spectrum colors), found at Ylijärvy, Finland. S.G. ~ 2.7; H = 6–6.5; R.I. ~ 1.55.

Spectroscopic: related to the spectrum or spectroscopy. The spectrum is a band of colors combined in white light (spectral colors), which are dispersed and appear side by side (red—orange—yellow—green—blue—violet) when the white light is refracted or diffracted. Each of these colors corresponds to a certain wavelength. During the transit of white light through a colored substance certain wavelengths are destroyed (absorbed), so that their absence from the spectrum leaves black lines or bands (absorption spectrum), which serve to identify the coloring element (spectroscopy; absorption spectroscopy) in gemstones.

Spessartite: transparent, orange-colored manganese aluminium garnet $Mn_3Al_2(SiO_4)_3$, with very high luster. S.G. = 4.16; H = 7; R.I. = 1.80.

Sphalerite: uncommon gemstone (collectors' stone) with the miners' name of zinc blend; yellow, orange, green; transparent with submetallic luster. ZnS. S.G. = 4.09; H = 3.5; R.I. = 2.37.

Sphene: transparent, much sought after, uncommon gemstone (collectors' stone) of yellow, green, and brown colors, with very high optical properties. Resinous to adamantine luster. $CaSiTiO_5$. S.G. = 3.53; H = 5.5; R.I. = 1.96.

Spherulite: ball-like mineral aggregate with radial structure.

Spinel: important but fairly rare gemstone, which occurs sparingly in large crystals but in all colors except yellow, brown, and green. Thanks to its high optical properties and hardness as well as its lack of cleavage, it is admirably suited for a gemstone. $MgAl_2O_4$. S.G. = 3.6–4.06; H = 8; R.I. = 1.717–1.78.

Spodumene: uncommon gemstone (collectors' stone) best known by its pink-lilac colored representative, kunzite, which owes its color to the pigment manganese. Much sought after is the green hiddenite, colored by chromium. Spodumene belongs to the large mineral group of the pyroxenes, and is thus related to jadeite (q.v.). $LiAlSi_2O_6$. S.G. = 3.18; H = 7; R.I. = 1.67.

Stalagmite: column-shaped rock formation of carbonate of lime, built up from the ground by water dripping from the roof in caves.

Star stone: general term for a gemstone with asterism, i.e. with a light effect resembling a star.

Stoichiometric: conforming to the condition of the equivalent weight.

Substitutional = replacing. An atom or a group of atoms that replaces other atoms or groups of atoms in an atomic lattice without destroying it.

Syenite: intermediate plutonic igneous rock, similar to granite; differentiated from granite by its poverty in quartz. Used as building and paving stone, also as an ornamental stone.

Synthetic: artificially manmade stones, manufactured by chemical/

technological processes, but having the same chemical, structural, and physical properties as the natural counterparts (e.g. synthetic ruby). They may be distinguished from the genuine gemstones by their inclusions.

Tetragonal = four-sided. The tetragonal crystal system comprises all those crystal classes which are characterized by an axial cross of two equal horizontal axes at right angles to each other and one vertical fourfold principal axis perpendicular to them.

Tetrahedron: crystal form of the cubic crystal system, bounded by four equilateral triangles. The basic structural form (unit cell) of the diamond corresponds to the tetrahedron.

Thorium: radioactive element; symbol Th; silver-gray, shiny, soft ductile metal. Half-life of the isotope Th 232 = $1,39.10^{10}$ years.

Tiger's eye: yellow to yellow-brown, silken lustered ornamental variety of cryptocrystalline (q.v.) quartz with cat's-eye effect (= chatoyancy (q.v.)) caused by fine parallel fibers of quartz pseudomorphs (q.v.) after crocidolite (a variety of hornblende). S.G. = 2.6; H = 7; R.I. = 1.53.

Titanium: chemical element, symbol Ti; silvery-white, easily malleable metal; it is the color-determining trace element in blue sapphire.

Titanite or *Sphene:* transparent, unusual gemstone; much sought after (collector's stone), colored yellow, green or brown, having very high optical properties. Brilliancy: from resinous to diamond-like. $CaSiTiO_5$. S.G. = 5.53; H = 5.5; R.I. = 1.96.

Topaz: important gemstone of striking clarity and transparency; colorless, yellow, golden brown, reddish brown, pale blue, rose-red to wine-red. Easy cleavage parallel to the basal plane. $F_2Al_2SiO_4$. S.G. = 3.53–3.56; H = 8; R.I. = 1.62–1.63. The name topaz is often used incorrectly for yellow to brown heat-treated amethyst, so-called citrine.

Tourmaline: popular gemstone, crystallizing in the trigonal system. Complex boro-aluminium-silicate which comprises the following important color varieties: achroite (colorless), dravite (brown), indicolite (blue), rubellite (pink to red), schorl (black), siberite (lilac to violet), and verdellite (green of all shades). Strongly pleochroic. S.G. = 3.05; H = 7; R.I. = 1.63.

Trachyte rock: gray or reddish, recent extrusive rock (extrusive equivalent of syenite (q.v.)) composed essentially of alkalic feldspar and minor biotite hornblende; forms sheets, veins, dome-shaped peaks or flows.

Transparency: ability to be seen through; often, too, degree of translucency.

Trap cut: rectangular style of cutting (or cut), mainly for colored stones (occasionally for diamond, too), in which the facets run parallel to the sides of the rectangular table. The number of steps on the pavilion is generally greater than that of the crown.

Triclinic = thrice inclined. The triclinic crystal system comprises all those crystal classes which are characterized by an axial intersection with three axes of unequal length and crossing one another at oblique angles.

Trigonal = three-sided. The trigonal crystal system comprises all those crystal classes which are characterized by an axial cross with one threefold main axis and three equal horizontal axes intersecting one another at an angle of 120 degrees in one plane.

Turquoise: opaque, mostly cryptocrystalline, compact ornamental stone of pale to deep blue or greenish blue color. Often porous; frequently interspersed by veins of dark brown limonite matrix. Hydrous copper-aluminium phosphate. S.G. = 2.6–2.8; H = 6; R.I. = 1.61.

Uranium: radioactive element; symbol U; silvery-white, heavy metal. Protomatter of various decay series, which are used in mineralogy and petrology for determining the age of rocks and mineral deposits.

Vanadium: chemical element; symbol V; hard, brittle, zinc-gray lustrous metal. Often the trace element which determines the color saturation or even the shaded hue in certain gemstones (ruby, emerald, tourmaline).

Wash: loose surface deposits of usually waterborne sands, clays, and pebbles as well as gravel and boulders, in which minerals resistant to weathering and mechanical transport, such as gemstones (gem wash or gem gravels) and precious metals, become concentrated and are therefore often exploitable.

Zircon: transparent colorless, yellow, brown, green, blue-green, blue and red gemstone, with high optical properties, so that the colorless variety in some respects resembles diamond, with traces of thorium (q.v.) and uranium (q.v.). Zirconium silicate $ZrSiO_4$. S.G. = 4.0–4.69; H = 6.5–7.5; R.I. = 1.79–1.98.

Zoisite: mineral family, named after Baron Zois von Edelstein, Slovenian nobleman, with several varieties used as gem and ornamental stones. Nontransparent pink thulite, colored by manganese. Nontransparent, green zoisite colored by chromium, combined with hornblende, forms anyolite, the unique mother rock of ruby, near Longido, Tanzania (zoisite rock). Transparent blue, pink, brown or violet strontium-bearing zoisite (sometimes called "tanzanite"). $Ca_2Al_3Si_3O_{12}OH$. S.G. = 3.25–3.37; H = 6.0–6.5; R.I. = 1.700–1.706.